SOCIAL SECURITY
for the
CLUELESS

SOCIAL SECURITY
for the
CLUELESS

DIANA ROSEN

Citadel Press
Kensington Publishing Corp.
http://www.kensingtonbooks.com

CITADEL PRESS BOOKS are published by
Kensington Publishing Corp.
850 Third Avenue
New York, NY 10022

All Kensington titles, imprints, and distributed lines are available at special
quantity discounts for bulk purchases for sales promotions, premiums, fund-
raising, educational, or institutional use. Special book excerpts or customized
printings can also be created to fit specific needs. For details, write or phone
the office of the Kensington special sales manager: Kensington Publishing
Corp., 850 Third Avenue, New York, NY 10022, attn: Special Sales
Department, phone 1-800-221-2647.

Citadel Press and the Citadel Logo are trademarks of
Kensington Publishing Corp.

First printing: June 2002

10 9 8 7 6 5 4 3 2 1

Printed in the United States of America

Library of Congress Control Number: 2001099193

ISBN: 0-8065-2317-4

To the helpful staff of the Social Security Administration,
who, with courtesy and grace,
serve the needs of beneficiaries one and all

This law represents a cornerstone in a structure that is being built but is by no means completed—a structure intended to lessen the force of possible future depressions, to act as a protection to future administrations of the Government against the necessity of going deeply into debt to furnish relief to the needy—a law to flatten out the peaks and valleys of deflation and of inflation—in other words, a law that will take care of human needs and at the same time provide for the United States an economic structure of vastly greater soundness.

—President Franklin Delano Roosevelt, August 14, 1935, on the enactment of the Social Security Administration law

Contents

CONTENTS

Preface

What should the words Social Security mean to you? Is it a windfall or a guaranteed retirement package? Is it a guaranteed specific amount? Is it all you need to retire?

The answer to all those questions is no. Social Security, for most workers, is an insurance plan to which you pay "premiums" in the form of taxes (that acronym FICA on your check stub each payday). Both how long you work and how much you make determine how much you will receive in benefits when you retire. But that's not all.

Social Security is more than a retirement package. It's a valuable umbrella of programs to help you and your spouse during your retirement, and after your death, to help your surviving spouse, children, and, in some cases, even your parents. Plus, auxiliary Social Security programs supplement income if you become indigent, and support you and your family during times when you or your family members sustain short- or long-term disability, making typical employment impossible.

Will funds for your Social Security benefits run out before YOU retire? The answer is no. The fund has, and will maintain, *trillions* of dollars. So when you read about six million dollars here and nine million dollars there being siphoned off, it barely affects the overall account. That does not mean that Social Security funds should be tampered with. Only your objections can make sure that Social Security monies are used only for their intended purpose.

Can Congress do away with Social Security? Anything is possible, but as is true for all privileges and rights that we have here in the United States, the price is eternal vigilance. We must pay constant attention to what our representatives are doing or want to be doing about issues related to the Social Security Administration.

You have an awesome amount of power, not only to vote your government officials out of office when adverse decisions impact your future, but to impeach them, protest against them, and make their office staff go nuts dealing with your emails, phone calls, letters, faxes, and personal visits to offices in the local district and in Washington, D.C.

In Appendix II, the current members and their contact information are listed. Put this list in your address book. Whenever you have a concern about Social Security, voice your concern. Tell everyone and anyone you know to do the same. Your Senator and Representative will pay attention to you, and if they do not, vote 'em out of office!

★   ★   ★

If you're self-employed, you have made all your contributions to the Social Security fund; if you're employed by someone else, you have paid about half, and your employer pays the other half. So, in essence, it is indeed your money in the Social Security fund. You deserve to get the return on your investment just like any similar financial vehicle.

It's hard to imagine, but until just before World War II, the many of the social and retirement benefits we now take for granted simply did not exist—especially Social Security, which only began in 1935.

Since 1937, the Social Security Administration (SSA) has expanded its role from primarily a retirement program to a government agency that actively responds to the needs of our minors, aged, disabled, and ill. The SSA helps more people than ever before both before and after retirement. For example:

- Minors can now receive benefits from the earnings of a parent upon his or her death or permanent disability.
- Spouses, including those divorced after ten years of marriage, are eligible for benefits.
- A worker's family may get a modest amount toward burial expenses.
- The disabled, blind, or otherwise physically compromised now have free vocational training and assistance finding a job.

DISABILITY

Perhaps no program administered by the SSA is as far-reaching or as immediately beneficial as the disability program, which helps millions of workers who, through illness or accident, are no longer able to work full-time and permanently. Disability also provides both services and financial assistance to families with children born with disabling conditions or for adults who are eager to work but who must leave the workplace frequently to accommodate the demands of their fragile physical or mental health.

MEDICARE

Another dramatic change in Social Security services is in the health insurance program, known as Medicare, which was created barely forty years ago (in 1965) to help both retirees and the disabled meet their growing medical needs.

SSI

The Supplemental Security Income program (SSI) assists the poorest retirees, disabled, and children by providing extra money and services to help them to achieve a more stable life.

INTERPRETATION AND COMMUNICATION

Among its auxiliary services, the SSA provides interpretation services for those for whom English is a second language. The SSA publications have been translated and printed in up to fifteen languages, including TTY phone systems and sign language for the deaf or hard-of-hearing. And, an interpreter can be provided to help anyone who is seeking SSA services in person.

The SSA has an all-inclusive Web site (www.ssa.gov) with pages available in Spanish and sections devoted to women. It operates more than 1,300 offices to serve people in person, and has both automated phones for 24-hour service, and personally staffed phone service (800-772-1213) to accommodate taxpayers twelve hours a day, five days a week.

OTHER SERVICES

SSA short- and long-term services aid new immigrants, and for those who, because of mental or physical problems, cannot provide for themselves. It provides assistance for families in transition who need a hand-up versus a handout, and for those affected by HIV/AIDS and domestic violence. And if you choose to live or travel extensively outside the U.S., the SSA has set up programs to ensure that your retirement benefits follow you wherever you go. The SSA has linked up with other governmental agencies that manage a wide range of social services from housing or home care to food stamps and counseling for the ill and the aging.

Social Security benefits have enabled many people to live during retirement or times of disability with more dignity, and a little more cash. In fact that "cash" amounts to nearly $6 *trillion* in retirement benefits paid since 1937.

The first step to unraveling the mystery of Social Security is buying this helpful guide. The next is to read through it to find all the information you need to know about Social Security—how it works, how to apply for its benefits, and how to ensure that your beneficiaries get their fair share.

SOCIAL SECURITY
for the
CLUELESS

1
HOW TO APPLY FOR A SOCIAL SECURITY CARD

TO EARN SOCIAL SECURITY *BENEFITS,* YOU *MUST* HAVE A SOCIAL SECURITY NUMBER

A Social Security number (SSN) is like a fingerprint; it is exclusively yours, and it will be a means of identification throughout your life. Your SSN is the primary piece of information the Social Security Administration (SSA) will use to help you receive all benefits due to you anytime you need them. And upon your death, your SSN is the key to providing your survivors with the benefits they need.

If you already have an SSN, it is important to update certain information, from address changes to name changes should you legally change your first or last name. The most common example of changing names is when men or women marry. (Yes, some men change their names when they marry. Life is full of options!)

The SSA has created a simple way to verify the information on your account. Each year you will receive a Statement of Earnings Report from the SSA, usually within three months of your birthday. Upon receipt, read it to make sure your name, address, and earnings are accurate. Any uncorrected errors could mean a loss of benefits later on or cause undue delays.

The SSA has a form or application for every service it offers. *Application for a Social Security Card* (SS-5), can be used by anyone who has never been issued a card, needs a replacement card, or has changed his or her name.

> **If you need to replace a lost Social Security card, change the name shown on the SSA card, or request a replacement card, you should use the same procedure: Complete Form SS-5. It is available for download at http://www.ssa.gov/online/ss-5.html or call 1-800-772-1213 or visit the SSA local Social Security office. The deaf or hard of hearing may call the TTY number, 800-325-0778.**

To change your address, get Form 8822, *Change of Address,* by calling 800-772-1213 or visiting your local SSA office, or access the downloadable change-of-address form at www.ssa.gov/mystatement/irscoa.htm.

WHERE TO SEND FORMS

After completing the form, take it to your nearest Social Security office. Be sure to take the originals or certified copies of your supporting documents along with the form.

To mail in your application and originals, send them by Registered or Certified Mail for safety and security. The SSA will return your original documents right away and your Social Security card will arrive in about two weeks.

Not sure where your local office is located?

Contact the Social Security Office Locator service online at www.ssa.gov/locator or call 800-772-1213 or write to the SSA at:

> Social Security Administration
> Office of Public Inquiries
> 6401 Security Boulevard
> Room 4-C-5 Annex
> Baltimore, MD 21235-6401

APPLYING FOR A SOCIAL SECURITY NUMBER ONLINE

Using the SSA Web site to apply for a Social Security card is easy, saves time, and gives you a head start on the process. However, "applying" is a misnomer. What you are doing is (1) obtaining an application form online and (2) filling it out online. You must still deliver the application to a local office or mail it *with original documents*. All the requested documents will be returned. You can download the application for a Social Security number at www.ssa.gov/online/ss-5 html.

Original documents will help verify your age, identity, and U.S. citizenship (or lawful alien status). Copies, certified by the custodian of the record, may be acceptable. After following the procedure below, your card will be mailed to you in about two to three weeks. Most delays occur because some document has not been received.

To prove your identity, bring any or all of the following:

1. a birth certificate or hospital record of your birth, if made before you were five years old, or a religious record such as a baptismal record if made before you were three months old. If you were born outside the United States, a current passport is acceptable.
2. driver's license
3. marriage or divorce record
4. military records, as applicable

As needed:

1. employer ID card
2. adoption record
3. life insurance policy
4. passport
5. health Insurance card (not a Medicare card)
6. school ID card

U.S. citizens born outside the United States require a U.S. consular report of birth, a U.S. passport, a Certificate of Citizenship, or a Certificate of Naturalization.

Alien residents born outside the United States require a current document issued to you by the U.S. Immigration and Naturalization Service (INS), such as Form I-551, I-94, I-688B, or I-766. A receipt for application is not evidence enough.

Not authorized to work in the United States? The SSA has made provisions so you can obtain a Social Security card; however, it will clearly show you still *cannot* work in the United States. The card can help you get other documents. You must prove your legal entry into the country for a valid *nonwork* reason, for example, being married to a U.S. citizen.

Mail or bring the application and evidence in person to your local Social Security office.

CLUE: Need to find out where your local Social Security office is? Access www.ssa.gov/locator or call toll-free 800-772-1213.

Complete the SS-5 using the instructions that come with it. Gather the required documents to prove your identity or that of your child and take it to the nearest Social Security office, or mail it to them. Take or mail *only originals or certified copies* of your documents, which will be returned to you immediately. The Social Security card will arrive by mail in about two weeks.

MAJOR CLUE: The SSA cannot, to date, accept online applications sent by WebTV or Mac computers, although it is making every effort to engage them in the Internet dialogue. Access www.ssa.gov to discover when they will accept WebTV or Mac users. Until then, you must use a computer with a PC platform, and it must be attached to a working printer.

DEATH

Timing is everything. In SSA terms, you have to die on schedule to have benefits paid to your spouse or dependent children. Because Social Security benefits are paid for the month prior to the date of the benefits check, benefits will always begin at least one month *after* the death. For example, if a beneficiary died anytime in July, the payment dated June 3 (that is, payment for July) must be returned. The first payment, then, will be July 3, which will be payment for August, the month *after* the worker died.

2
WHAT EVERYONE SHOULD KNOW ABOUT SOCIAL SECURITY

Numerous phone calls to countless field offices, regional offices, and communications with both offline and on-line sources have convinced me that the Social Security Administration is definitely on our side.

The staff is well trained and well informed; courteous in answering any questions; and able to provide pamphlets, on-the-spot verbal information, referrals to other sources, and other material to help you become informed about your Social Security benefits package. The SSA handles, literally, millions of phone calls, so it's not unexpected that you might wait for a response.

However, if you call during midweek off-hours, and are well prepared to ask your questions, the process will go considerably quicker and smoother. The best thing is that all personal assistance and information provided by the SSA is *free*.

MAJOR CLUE: Social Security is not just about retirement benefits. It's a whole lot more.

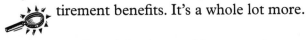

Certainly, it provides a modest pension to anyone who has contributed to the program for a minimum amount of time. It also pays benefits to eligible widows and widowers, to minor children of deceased workers, and to disabled workers and disabled children who qualify for the program.

Since the mid-1960s, Social Security has also provided medical coverage via Medicare, and Supplemental Security Income to the indigent, ill, or needy. And most recently the SSA has introduced the Ticket to Work Program, employment training for the disabled, which enables qualified workers to earn more than their SSA benefits would pay, and contributes to their dignity, self-esteem, and productivity.

Throughout each chapter, references are made to specific pamphlets, forms, and brochures the SSA has published. You can obtain these materials by:

1. calling toll free 800-772-1213
2. visiting the Web site at www.ssa.gov/
3. visiting or writing your local or field SSA office

CLUE: If you don't have a personal computer, you can use one free at many public libraries and various nonprofit organizations that provide computer use for the public. If you are already a beneficiary or will soon be one, put the SSA phone number on a label and stick it onto your telephone, and if you use a computer, put these numbers on a label and put it on the frame of your monitor. You will refer to this information a lot!

ORIGIN OF SOCIAL SECURITY

The term "Social Security" was first used in the United States by Abraham Epstein in connection with his group, the American Association for Social Security. Originally, the Social Security Act of 1935 was named the Economic Security Act, but this title was changed during Congressional consideration of the bill.

WHO BENEFITS FROM SOCIAL SECURITY?

You do! Social Security offers benefits to every man, woman, and child in the United States, depending upon need.

Retirees

Retirement benefits from Social Security continue to increase, although they are still modest. Some indigent retirees depend on their Social Security benefits to cover everything from food to rent to daily expenses.

The Disabled, Ill, and Indigent

Today, if you become disabled, chronically ill, or indigent, the SSA has a program or two to help you, including Disability Insurance, Medicare, Supplemental Social Insurance, vocational training, Social Security benefits for your children, and links to other agencies that provide services on either the local or the state level where you live.

Women

Many women do double duty: they work *and* they serve as the primary caregivers for children, ill or aged parents, and ill or aged spouses. These women are responsible for the disbursement of benefits for their charges, so their personal lives involve not only the attention to the emotional and physical needs of their families, but management of financial needs and services, too. Becoming a caregiver may necessitate leaving the workforce in favor of family needs, so women's total contributions to their own SSA retirement package are less consistent than most men's. Many women now earn more individual benefits than spousal benefits, and this trend is growing.

Children

A variety of SSA programs, from medical care to financial support, are designed to help children who are born with life-threatening diseases or lifelong conditions that make them unable to participate in the workforce, or to help families plagued by poverty, illness, or the death of a worker.

BENEFITS CAN BE TAXED! (OR, TAXES DON'T END WITH RETIREMENT)

In an ideal world, receiving Social Security benefits should be simply getting a check each month for benefits earned and that's that. Not so. Your benefits can be offset by pensions (see chapter 10), they can be taxed because you earn too much other income, or they can be offset by income tax owed. Fortunately, there is a small amount (15 percent) that you are always allowed to keep. Since the average check is about $700, that means you could be taxed as much as $595, and be left with $105. This amount should help in understanding why financial planning, numbers crunching, and decision making about working vs. not working at retirement age are so critical!

The key to determining how much of the 85 percent of your benefits check can be taxed rests on how much "combined income" you have vs. how much you receive in benefits. "Combined income" is your adjusted gross income *plus* nontaxable interest *plus* one half of your Social Security benefits.

If you file a federal income tax return as an individual and your combined income is $25,000 to $34,000, you may have to pay up to 50 percent of your Social Security benefits. For example, if your Social Security benefits are $700, you may be taxed on $350 of that amount. If your combined income exceeds $44,000, you may have to pay up to 85 percent of your Social Security benefits. For example, if your Social Security benefits are $700, you may be taxed on $595 of that amount.

Even if you file a separate return as a married person, you may need to pay taxes on your Social Security benefits if your income exceeds the SSA limit for how much you can earn at your age.

If you file a federal income tax return as a joint tax return and the combined incomes are $32,000 to $44,000, you may have to pay taxes on up to 50 percent of your Social Security benefits. For example, if your Social Security benefits are $700, you may be taxed on $350 of that amount.

If you are not a U.S. citizen nor a resident, federal income taxes will be automatically withheld from your benefits at a rate of 30 percent of 30 percent of your benefit amount. If, for example, your benefit amount is $700, you will be taxed 30 percent of $210 or $63.

Good news! After age 70, your combined retirement income is no longer a factor in the taxation of your SSA retirement benefits. You may keep all the SSA benefit even if you win the lottery.

Federal income taxes will be withheld from the benefits of all nonresident aliens, except those who reside in countries that have tax treaties with the United States that do not permit taxing of U.S. Social Security benefits (or provide for a lower tax rate). Those countries are Canada, Egypt, Germany, Ireland, Israel, Italy, Japan, Romania, Switzerland, and the United Kingdom.

MAJOR CLUE: It would be a blessing to live long enough to receive all the benefits and interest that you or you and your employer contributed via the FICA tax. That scenario is not always possible, so it's more realistic to consider Social Security an addendum to your retirement plan, not the whole of it. Social Security benefits are helpful during retirement, but they rarely cover all of anyone's financial needs, nor will they always catch up to the rising costs of everyday expenses.

The opportunities for savings and investments are

many, and the key is to save and invest regularly and consistently throughout your working life. Read up on the best choices or consider such classic investments as stocks, bonds, savings bonds, certificates of deposit, real estate, business investments—or marrying someone rich.

3
PREPARING YOUR PERSONAL SSA FILE FOR LIFE

MAJOR CLUE: Prepare now for retirement later. Ideally, the time to prepare for retirement and to track your Social Security contributions should begin the very first day of the very first job you take. Whether you're a teenager or reentering the workforce in midlife, or facing retirement age in a few months, the best time to prepare and plan for retirement is *today*.

And the very first thing to do is to create your Personal SSA File for Life. You will most likely only have to gather all the required papers once. Subsequent updates for changes or additions as your life itself changes will take only a few minutes of your time. When you file for retirement benefits, or if you should need Medicare, SSI, or other SSA-related benefits for you or your family, having all the necessary records at your fingertips will speed up the process of receiving benefits, and make it easier on you and your beneficiaries.

WHAT YOU NEED IN YOUR SSA FILE

To fulfill most of the requests made by the SSA, you must show *originals* of important papers, not photocopies, notarized statements, faxes, or e-mailed copies. The only exception is a certified copy from the custodian of record at your city's Hall of Records, Department of Vital Statistics, military service headquarters, or comparable agency.

Because these papers are so important, they must be readily available. Delays in providing them to the SSA will mean delays in receiving benefits. Among the papers you should always keep in your Personal SSA File for Life are:

Birth Certificate

If you do not have yours, write to the department of Vital Statistics in the state where you were born (see listing in Appendix I) and request a certified copy from the Custodian of Record. All of these departments charge a nominal fee for the service, and it's a good idea to call to verify the current amount rather than just sending in a check with your letter.

When calling to request a certified copy of your birth certificate, ask the clerk:

1. the current fee
2. what identification papers or information is required to receive your copy
3. whether a discount is available for multiple copies if, for example, your spouse or representative payee also needs a copy

4. whether anything else is necessary to acquire your certified copy

Although these workers provide information daily, it's always a good idea for them to double-check with you to make sure all your obligations are listed. This can save time and energy and can also eliminate repeated phone calls later on.

CLUE: If you were born in the town where you now live, check for Vital Statistics in the "County Government" listings at the front of your telephone book. To find out the location of a Vital Statistics department online, access www.cdc.gov/nchs/ howto/w2w/ alphabet.htm.

Keep the phone number and address of the Vital Statistics office in a separate file or address book. If you put information related to your birth certificate on your computer, make a backup disk and store it in a safe place, away from both the SSA file and your information file.

CLUE: In some cases a baptismal certificate may be acceptable in place of a birth certificate. Always check with the SSA representative to find out whether this is so in your case.

Military Discharge Papers (as Applicable)

All veterans, male and female, should keep their military discharge papers. Getting additional copies of military discharge papers takes a really long time, so if you don't have copies, request them *now*.

The Department of Veterans Affairs does *not* maintain records! So don't ask them. But the following agency will assist you in obtaining copies of separation papers from any of the branches of the U.S. Armed Forces, if you do not have the originals.

Armed forces personnel information is maintained by the Military Personnel Records Center in St. Louis, part of the National Archives and Records Administration, accessed at www.nara.gov/regional/mpr.html, or write directly to:

> National Personnel Records Center
> ATTN: Military Personnel Records Center
> 9700 Page Boulevard
> St. Louis, MO 63132-5100

Send your request as a letter. And be patient. Turnaround times for records requested vary greatly. The NPRC Military Records Facility currently holds more than 70 million records on file! To speed up the request process, please provide as much information as you can in your letter. Currently there is a backlog of over 200,000 requests, and approximately 5,000 new ones are received *daily*. Routine requests for separation statements require four to five weeks for servicing and the average turnaround time on all requests is from three and one-half to four months.

A serious fire occurred at the center in 1973, so any requested records related to that time period take even longer to process. Unlike the SSA, the NPRC does not require originals, so you can send them copies of important papers needed to obtain your military discharge papers, such as those listed below.

DISCHARGE INFORMATION REQUEST

Request *Report of Separation from Active Duty*, #DD-214.

The following basic information is of paramount importance:

1. veteran's complete name used while in service
2. service number or Social Security number
3. branch of service, and dates for beginning and ending of service period

The following information is helpful but not always necessary:

1. date and place of birth
2. place of discharge
3. last unit of assignment
4. place of entry into the service, if known

You can also read *Requests for Veterans' Military Information* at www.va.gov/vas/pafoia.html. This Web page gives instructions for submitting an SF 180 *Request Pertaining to Military Records*.

The National Military Personnel Records Center has the SF 180 form that you can download at www.nara.gov/regional/mprsf180.html. The SF 180 may be photocopied as needed, but you must submit a separate request (either SF 180 or a letter) for each individual whose records are requested. You may submit more than one request per envelope by mail, or fax them to:

> National Personnel Records Center
> Military Personnel Records
> 9700 Page Avenue
> St. Louis, MO 63132-5100
> Fax: 314-538-4175

The center will respond in writing by mail. At this printing, requests for discharge papers are not accepted over the Internet because of privacy and security issues and susceptibility to unauthorized use or fraud.

OTHER WAYS TO OBTAIN THE SF 180 FORM
You can access the SF 180 from the National Archives and Records Administration's Fax-on-Demand system. Using the handset, call the system from a fax machine and follow the voice-activated instructions. This service is *free*, except for any long-distance telephone charges you may incur on your fax phone. The fax number is 301-713-6905.

CLUE: The SF 180 document is known as Document Number 2255 on the NARA Fax-on-Demand system.

Your nearest Veterans Administration (VA) regional office can send you Standard Form 180, *Request Pertaining to Military Records* (SF 180), when you call them toll-free at 800-827-1000.

When you receive your new copies of military discharge papers, put them in your file, and keep the above access information in a separate file or address book, along with your service record number. If you put information about your military service on your computer, make a backup disk and store it in a safe place, away from both the SSA file and your information file.

Certificates of Marriage and Divorce or Annulment (as Applicable)

No matter how often or how long ago you were married or divorced, you must keep all records because they will affect both your benefits payments and those of your spouse or ex-spouse, especially if the marriage was a long one. Divorced couples married ten years or longer may be eligible for benefits on their ex-spouse's records. Husbands can claim on wives' records and wives on husbands' records, as eligible.

If you do not have your papers, write to the Hall of Records where you registered your marriage or where the divorce was decreed, and obtain certified copies. Most Halls of Records charge a nominal fee, so call first to find out what the obligations are. You will probably be asked the basic information, e.g., names and birthdates of the couple, city of marriage registry, date of wedding. Before hanging up, always ask if there is any other information the clerk needs or if there is any more information you need to expedite the request.

Some states have all records in one place, but most of them delegate the record keeping of registrations of marriage certificates and licenses, and divorce decrees, to the counties that issued them. (See the Vital Statistics directory in Appendix I for more information.)

If you were married and/or divorced in the county where you now live, check the "County Government" listings in the front of your telephone book for the phone number.

Keep the Hall of Records phone number and address in a separate file or address book. If you put information about marriages or divorces on your computer, make a backup disk and store it in a safe place, away from both the SSA file and your information file.

Papers for Your Children, Natural or Adopted

You should always have the birth certificates, Social Security numbers, and adoption records, as applicable, for all your children. If the children are adults but disabled, you should always keep the records or assign them to your legal representative or accountant. If the children are adults but still dependent upon you financially and/or are living with you, you should also keep their papers. Otherwise, you may choose to give these important papers to your children when they come of age.

If your spouse has the original marriage and/or divorce papers, whether you're living together or separated, you should make copies for your own records, and make a note of the phone number and address of the Hall of Records or Vital Statistics department where your children are registered. Keep this information in a separate file or address book, and if you put it on your computer, make a backup disk and store it in a safe place, away from both the SSA file and your information file.

This is particularly important for parents of minors. If you are the only parent living (or the only one engaged in the management and care of minor children), it is important that a relative, representative payee, or lawyer have copies of these papers, in case of your incapacity or death.

Spousal Information

While your spouse (or ex-spouse) should keep the originals of his or her own important papers, you should have his or her vital statistics written down or copies of papers, plus any and all phone numbers, addresses, and key identification numbers; birth, marriage, divorce, and death certificates; and documents for the children of each spouse and ex-spouse. Social Security numbers should be listed for all spouses and ex-spouses. Your lawyer or accountant may keep these for you.

Other Important Papers

You may carry some or all of the following identification papers in your wallet. They should be copied and placed in your SSA file, too, along with related phone numbers and addresses to obtain replacement copies, should your wallet be lost or stolen. They include:

1. driver's license
2. employer ID card
3. passport
4. health insurance cards that are *not* Medicare cards
5. school ID cards for dependent children

WHERE TO KEEP YOUR SSA FILE

Treat your SSA file like gold, because it is certainly the key to getting the "gold" when you're eligible to receive your benefits. Keep the file in a safe-deposit box or a locked, fireproof file cabinet. And inform your spouse, lawyer, executor, or a trustworthy friend where these papers are located.

Review the file each year on a significant day, such as your birthday, anniversary, April fifteenth, or another day that is important to you. This yearly review is the time to maintain, update, or add new information. It takes but a few minutes and will save you hours of paperwork, phone calls, and "hunting" when you need these documents the most.

If you prefer, you can store this information with your advocate or representative payee, lawyer, accountant, executor, or a bank trustee, but *always* update it yearly.

CLUE: Rules vary from bank to bank about access, especially with safe-deposit boxes, so check to see if your chosen representative may access the box for you should you be incapacitated or upon your death. If he or she will not have access to the box, choose an alternative storage source such as a security file kept by an attorney, accountant, or trusted associate or friend.

LEARN HOW TO ASK QUESTIONS ON YOUR OWN BEHALF

As a journalist, I've learned that *how* you ask a question is the most important key to obtaining the information you need, and planning your questions makes you a successful interviewer. What follows is a little question primer that can save you lots of time and frustration, and will get you the information you need quickly and easily.

Although I've asked most of these questions and provided their answers here, the samples below are meant to explain how to ask questions particular to your individual needs. There are many variables related to earnings, marital history, health, and other circumstances that may affect the amount and the duration of your benefits, so if you do not see the answer to your question in this book, call the SSA office following these guidelines, and you will be an accomplished interviewer on your own behalf.

1. Be Prepared

Whether visiting an SSA office or calling for information, you need to be prepared with paperwork and your questions so that you do not wander off the topic, discuss personal situations that are best kept private, or lose the focus or purpose of your call. Always have your personal file of papers or a list of your primary "numbers" in front of you before making any call, especially your Social Security number or the SSN of the person for whom you're calling.

2. Interviews Are a Two-Way Conversation: Questions and Answers

To make your call to the SSA most effective, you should be as prepared to *answer* questions as you are prepared to ask them. Think about the possible questions the SSA would ask and gather as much information about yourself as you can. You know they'll ask for your identification information first: name, address, telephone, and always, your SSN. However, you should be prepared with bank information if you're calling about any aspect of direct deposit, or name, address, and telephone number when calling about a representative payee, for example. By having all this information, you can also verify that the SSA is current about any changes to your account.

3. Write Everything Down Before You Call

Keep index cards or a notebook near your phone with the basic information you will always need when calling the SSA. That information would be the same for you or the person you're calling for as a representative payee or spouse or child of elderly parents. The following is in addition to that listed above:

- birth information
- name, if you've changed it because of marriage or divorce, or for professional reasons
- death information, as necessary
- Medicare, SSI, or disability numbers, as applicable

- any other information related to your question, e.g., names and numbers of physicians, social workers, representative payees, or anyone or any service or institution you'd like to discuss

4. Think of Your Needs Before You Call

Write them down. Even keywords will help you frame questions if you do not want to write down exact questions. Some keywords might be *SSI, Medicare, disability benefits, retirement benefits, direct deposit,* or similar words that can help the agent assist you.

5. Edit Your Thoughts Down to a Topic Question

This is the real key to asking questions. It should begin with "I need information about . . ." Or "How can I . . ." Or if you're calling for someone else, for example, say, "I am a [spouse, representative payee, caregiver] for— and I need to know—" Your introductory questions should contain the keyword about your needs.

Here are some examples:

"I need information about obtaining the death benefit. Where can I get that information?"

"My Social Security card was stolen. How can I get it replaced?"

"My wife just died and I need to inform Social Security, can you help me?"

"I am the representative payee for a disabled child. I need to know how to report his change of address."

Stolen SSNs are frequently used to obtain credit card, bank account, tax, and even payroll information yet tracking and recovering from the abuse can be very difficult, so report the theft immediately.

6. Make the Call

Okay, you're prepared with questions and information, and you're ready to call. When the agent answers, ask your main questions. If framed as described above, the clerk will immediately know how to help you or will refer you to another agent who can.

Remember, there is no such thing as a stupid question, only people willing to be stupid rather than be informed. So, no matter how simple or complex your concerns are, ask questions to find out what you need to know.

When you are satisfied that you have the information you need, ask the clerk if she can think of anything else you need to know, or anything you need to follow up on at a later date. If you are being sent information, ask approximately when you will receive it.

Last, but certainly not least, thank the clerk for her assistance. She answers hundreds of calls a day; a little thanks is easy, costs nothing, and will bring a rich ray of acknowledgment to those who have served you.

Forgot to ask something? Thought of something completely off the topic? Call back. You may not be able to get the same agent, but you'll get your answer. It's always better to make a second or third call for additional information, than to remain ignorant of the answers that can help you get the most out of your benefits program.

MAJOR CLUE: When a spouse or a family member who is an SSA beneficiary dies, it is often difficult to do the ordinary, for the grief is so fresh that it may be impossible to remain unemotional enough to report the death to the SSA intelligently. The SSA understands that, so please allow a family member or friend to assist you. Of course, if you have a representative payee, that person can report the death. It should be done within ten days of the death.

There's no law that says you have to do everything yourself, especially during this critical time. However, the law does say that reporting the death of a beneficiary must be done immediately. The SSA may require repayment of benefits issued to the deceased at any time during the month he or she died. Failure to report the death means you not only have to return benefit money, but you may be charged interest or a fine. (No, it's not fair, but it's the law.)

"The Social Security program is the best expression of community that we have in this country today."

—Senator Bill Bradley (D-NJ), 1983

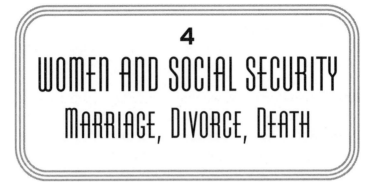

4
WOMEN AND SOCIAL SECURITY
MARRIAGE, DIVORCE, DEATH

... in the old days the individuals themselves would have been putting money away for their old age—and, as far as the present plan is concerned, that is actually what they are doing. The present plan is more secure because today the government receives the money and is back of it; and as long as the government is stable, they are sure of their old age insurance. They will not go through the tragedy of putting their money in a sock and then losing the sock or having it stolen, or of putting it in a bank run by individuals whose bad judgment sometimes made the bank fail. I do not think we have really changed the basic obligations in this case. We have simply made it a responsibility of government and thereby a little more secure for the individual.

From the "My Day" newspaper column written
by Former First Lady Eleanor Roosevelt, August 15, 1949

When I saw this bill adopted by Congress with a large majority of votes of both parties, and when I later saw, after a few flurries of opposition in later years, both parties continue to improve it and to broaden its coverage and to make more generous its benefits, I have come to realize that not only was it the crowning act of my work-

31

ing life, but that it was perhaps one of the most useful blessings which time has brought to the American people.

From the words of former U.S. Treasurer
Frances Perkins in 1960

In this new century, women in the United States still earn less than men overall and, therefore, often earn lower Social Security benefits than men. Women in the workplace have the same or more responsibility as men; however, most men have not as yet taken up the other roles women play as caregivers for frail parents, disabled children, or a disabled or retired spouse. Leaving the workplace for pregnancy or the early childrearing years also impacts the overall earned credits of many working women.

Perhaps it is all this added responsibility that has enabled women to live longer than men, for they represent 60 percent of all older Social Security beneficiaries and 72 percent of those 85 and older. Women's longevity is no small irony: They may not receive much in benefits per month, but they may receive more benefits over their longer lifetimes.

A woman who turns 65 this year is expected to live at least until age 84 or longer while a man who is 65 this year has a life expectancy of about 80. For both men and women, life expectancy is projected to increase in the next few decades.

Women, then, have longevity on their side; today's younger women have increased opportunities to work at better-paying jobs and have more cooperation in childrearing—and more women are staying in the workforce longer, and therefore earning more overall. Pension coverage for women is increasing and is now almost equal to that for men, but women's benefits continue to be lower because of their lower overall earnings. Most critically, more and more women are taking control of their own financial health, and making a lifelong commitment to overseeing their personal investments and savings.

Still, the poverty rate remains 13 percent for elderly women, almost double that of elderly men; and unmarried women are usually poorer than married or widowed women. The current SSA statistics are:

Marital Status of Women 65 or Older

1. Married: 5%
2. Divorced: 22%
3. Widowed: 18%
4. Never married: 20%

Women receive, on average, about $700 in monthly benefits, and most widows and other unmarried women age 65 and older (74 percent) depend upon Social Security for 50 percent or more of their total income. The picture for unmarried elderly women is sadder: 26 percent are dependent upon Social Security for their *entire* income.

In contrast, unmarried older men rely on their benefits for only 36 percent of their income. (Still-married couples use their benefits for 33 percent of their income.) Part of this inequity is based, as always, on the earnings of women in comparison to those of men. Women's earnings fall at least $10,000 short of the median average earnings for men ($27,000 compared to $37,000). Although women's earnings are increasing, they are still not up to speed with those of men, even with similar educations or skill levels, and women still do not work as many years, so they often do not earn as many credits as men.

It behooves every woman to oversee her own financial portfolio, especially in an era when more than half of all marriages end in divorce and nearly 17 percent of women will never marry.

What seems unlikely to change is women's caregiver role handling family finances, supervising child care, being responsible for long-term care for aging or ill parents, being responsible for adult disabled children, and the financial and medical needs for their spouses and themselves.

SURVIVORS BENEFITS

Although thousands of men collect benefits on their wives' Social Security contributions, it is the millions of women, both as caregivers of underage children and as eligible widows, who receive the bulk of Social Security benefits. Survivors who lose a family wage earner (male or female) from death not only experience the loss of their loved one, but also the loss of a steady income. It is rare that anyone is clear-headed during this period, and at such times the benefit of a well-prepared SSA file will be especially obvious.

When someone who has worked and paid into Social Security dies, survivors benefits may be paid to certain family members. These include widows, widowers (and divorced widows and widowers), children, and dependent parents. The total value of the survivors insurance you have under Social Security may be more than the value of your individual life insurance, although it is paid out in monthly benefits rather than a lump sum as from a traditional life insurance policy.

You, or your representative payee, should contact the SSA immediately to set the paperwork in action for your benefits while you go through the grief process as best you can. Your local SSA office can also refer you to social services you may need to help pull your family together. Call toll free at 800-772-1213. If you are deaf or hard of hearing, call the TTY number: 800-325-0778; both numbers are available 7 A.M. to 7 P.M. every business day.

CLUE: Your surviving spouse or your minor children may be eligible to receive a special onetime death payment of $255 that most families use toward burial expenses. Although this is a nominal amount, it is helpful and has no effect on any other benefits owed to survivors.

HOW SURVIVORS BENEFITS ARE EARNED

When you die, certain members of your family may be eligible for survivors benefits if you worked in a job or were self-employed and paid Social Security taxes and earned enough SSA-required credits. You can earn a maximum of 4 credits each year. The number of credits you earned, and your age at death, determine the amount that your survivors will receive when you die. The minimum amount of credits needed in most cases is 40. The younger a person is, the fewer credits he or she needs for family members to be eligible for survivors benefits.

CLUE: Under a special rule, benefits can be paid to your children and your spouse who is caring for the children, even if you have not acquired the requisite number of credits. They can get benefits if you have credit for one and one-half years of work in the three years just before your death. Today, 98 out of every 100 children are eligible for benefits if a working parent dies. In fact, Social Security pays more benefits to children than any other federal program.

WHO CAN GET SURVIVORS BENEFITS?

Survivors can be:

1. a widow or widower aged 60 to 65—Full benefits are paid to your widow or widower when they are age 65 or older or they may receive reduced benefits as early as age 60. Exceptions: A disabled widow or widower can get benefits if they are between 50 and 60 years old. The surviving spouse's benefits may be reduced if he or she also receives a pension from a job where Social Security taxes were not withheld.

2. a widow(er) at any age—Full benefits will be awarded to widowed spouses of any age provided they are the caregivers of children under 16 years old or of children who are disabled and received benefits because of their disability.

3. unmarried children under 18 (or up to age 19 if

they are attending elementary or secondary school full time) and children of any age if disabled before age 22 and still disabled when you file. Benefits may also be paid to stepchildren, grandchildren, and adopted children under certain circumstances.

4. dependent parents at 62 or older. If they rely upon their children's earnings for at least half of their personal income, they may receive SSA benefits upon the death of their children.

5. divorced spouses—If you've been divorced, your former spouse can get benefits under the same circumstances as your widow(er) if your marriage lasted 10 years or more. Your former spouse, however, does not have to meet the length-of-marriage rule if caring for your child who is under 16 years old or disabled and who is also getting benefits on your Social Security record. (The child must be your former spouse's natural or legally adopted child.)

CLUE: Benefits paid to a surviving divorced spouse who is age 60 or older (50 to 60 years old if disabled) will not affect the benefit rates for other survivors getting benefits.

WHAT IS A SPOUSE?

Social Security defines a spouse as someone who:

1. was legally married to a worker who earned benefits.

2. is a husband or wife listed on intestate personal property.
3. lived as a spouse with the worker in the same household when he or she applied for benefits (unless you were divorced from the worker at the time).
4. was married in a rite or ceremony that proved invalid under "applicable law" because of a prior marriage or its dissolution although you married the worker in good faith, and were not aware that any previous marriage or dissolution was invalid. ("Applicable law" is applied by the courts of the state where the insured worker lived when the spouse filed for benefits.) The District of Columbia does not recognize the applicable law ruling.

HOW TO APPLY FOR SURVIVORS BENEFITS

How you sign up for survivors benefits depends on whether or not you're already getting other Social Security benefits for yourself based on the work records of another spouse.

If You Aren't Getting Social Security Benefits

Whether or not you already receive any SS benefits, you should apply for survivors benefits promptly when a working spouse or parent dies, because in some cases benefits may not be retroactive. You can apply by telephone or at any Social Security office.

The SSA needs either original documents or copies certified by the agency that issued them including:

1. proof of death—either from funeral home or death certificate
2. your Social Security number, and that of the worker's
3. your birth certificate
4. your marriage certificate if you're a widow(er)
5. your divorce papers if you're applying as a surviving divorced spouse
6. dependent children's Social Security numbers
7. the deceased worker's W-2 Forms or federal self-employment tax return for the most recent year
8. the name of your bank and the account number where benefits will be deposited

CLUE: If you can't put your hands on all of these important papers, begin the application process anyway—some benefits are retroactive, while others are not.

HOW TO APPLY FOR SURVIVORS BENEFITS IF YOU ARE ALREADY RECEIVING SOCIAL SECURITY BENEFITS

A spouse can earn Social Security benefits several ways:

1. a *spousal* benefit, a portion of the retired worker's pension that is payable to a spouse
2. a *retired worker's* pension which you yourself have earned based on your work credits
3. a *survivors* benefit, payable to a widow(er) of a deceased worker

A survivor's pension nearly always exceeds a spousal benefit, but a survivor's pension may or may not exceed your own retirement pension.

If you are receiving spousal benefits based on a retiree's benefits and the retiree dies, report the death to the SSA immediately (within ten days). This is the only way the SSA can then change your payments, if you are eligible, to survivors benefits, which may be higher than spousal benefits. Benefits for any children will automatically be changed to survivors benefits after the death of the retired worker is reported to the SSA. You will be contacted by the SSA only if more information is needed.

If you are earning retirement benefits on your own record, you may be eligible for more money as a widow(er). Complete an *Application to Receive Survivors Benefits*, and attach the spouse's death certificate.

Some people may be able to file for retirement or survivors benefits over the phone. Call the toll-free number, 800-772-1213, to find out whether a phone call is enough to activate your request. Have the following items on hand when you call: your Social Security number, your birth certificate, your most recent W-2 Form or tax return, bank account numbers, and in the case of survivors benefits, the SSN of the deceased. If there are minor children eligible for survivors benefits, you will be asked for their SSNs.

HOW MUCH WILL MY BENEFITS BE?

The amount of benefits you can get is a percentage of the deceased's basic Social Security benefit. The percentage depends on your age and the type of benefit you are eligible for. For example:

1. A widow(er) age 65 or older will receive 100 percent of the spouse's Social Security benefit.
2. A widow(er) age 60 to 64 will receive 71 to 94 percent of the spouse's Social Security benefit.
3. A widow(er) of any age with a child under 16 will receive 75 percent of the spouse's Social Security benefit.
4. Children under the age of 18 will receive 75 percent of the spouse's Social Security benefit, although limits have been placed on the amount of money paid to survivors and their children. The limits impose a cap on how much a family can receive based on one deceased worker's benefit.

For example, a surviving spouse may receive 75 percent of the deceased worker's benefit and one child may receive 75 percent of the benefit, for a total of 150 percent. If there is a second, third, or more children, the family may receive as much as 30 percent more, up to a total of 180 percent of the deceased's benefit.

RETIREMENT BENEFITS FOR WIDOW(ERS)

If you are receiving widow(ers) benefits, whether you had been divorced from the deceased worker or not, you may switch to your own retirement benefit as early as age 62 if you're eligible and your retirement benefit is higher than your widow(er) rate. In many cases, a widow(er) can begin receiving one benefit at a reduced rate and then switch to the other benefit at an unreduced rate at age 65.

The rules are quite involved and more complicated than we can address here, so please contact your SSA representative before making any switch from widow(er) (spousal) benefits to your own. Call toll free 800-772-1213 between 7 A.M. and 7 P.M. on business days. If you are deaf or hard of hearing, you may call the toll-free TTY number, 800-325-0778, between 7 A.M. and 7 P.M. on business days, or visit your local SSA office.

SURVIVORS BENEFITS FOR PEOPLE WHO WORK

When you get Social Security survivors benefits, the amount may be reduced if your earnings exceed certain limits (changed yearly). These reductions apply only to workers under 69 years old. When you reach 70, there are no limits placed upon your earning and you can receive your entire Social Security benefit *package*. Because this package changes annually, read the leaflet *How Work Affects Your Benefits*, Publication No. 05-10069. Contact your local SSA office about your obligations if you have not already received a notice about earnings limits for the current year. Call toll free 800-772-1213 between 7 A.M. and 7 P.M. on business days. If you are deaf or hard of hearing, you may call the toll-free TTY number, 800-325-0778, between 7 A.M. and 7 P.M. on business days.

CLUE: If you earn survivors benefits, are working, and are under 69, your survivors benefits can be reduced but the benefits of other members of your family will *not* be affected.

WHAT IF A WIDOW(ER) REMARRIES?

From the SSA's point of view, it pays to wait for romance. You generally cannot get survivors benefits if you remarry, but if you rewed when you are older than 60 (or older than 50 if you are disabled), your survivors benefits will remain untouched. When you reach the age of 62, you may get benefits on the record of your *new* spouse if they are higher than those of your former spouse.

CLUE: Your personal information is safe with Social Security. The SSA does its best to keep all the information personal and confidential on the millions of people in their records. If you want someone else, like a representative payee, to help you with your Social Security transactions, the SSA needs *your permission* before releasing any information to him or her, or to anyone else. You need to be with your representative if you visit the SSA offices or you may send along a written consent letter. If your representative calls the SSA, you must be available to talk with an SSA representative during the time the call is placed, unless you are incapacitated. A natural parent or legal guardian can act on behalf of a minor child who earns Social Security benefits.

EXCEPTION: The law requires Social Security to give information to other government agencies operating health or welfare programs, such as Temporary Assistance to Needy Families, Medicaid, and food stamps. Agencies receiving information from Social Security are prohibited from sharing that information, and violations of this confidentiality are penalized.

Widow(er)s must meet certain criteria, which include the following:

1. You must be 60 years old or older.
2. If you are disabled (following the criteria for disabled), you must be at least 50 years old but not yet 60.
3. If you are widowed and disabled but between the ages of 60 and 64, you are entitled to disabled widow(er)s benefits for Medicare coverage.
4. The worker must have been fully insured upon death for you to earn benefits.
5. You are not entitled to a retirement insurance benefit that is equal to or larger than the worker's primary insurance amount.
6. You were married to the deceased worker for at least the nine months just before the worker died; in the month before the month you married the deceased worker you were entitled to disability benefits under the Social Security Act; or you were entitled to an insurance annuity under the Railroad Retirement Act.
7. You are the biological parent of the worker's son or daughter if a live child was born to you and the worker, even if the child did not survive.
8. You legally adopted the worker's child during your marriage and before the child reached age 18.
9. You were married to the worker when you both legally adopted a child under age 18.
10. The worker legally adopted your child dur-

ing your marriage and the child was then under age 18.

WHEN YOUR SPOUSE DIES

Widows and widowers are treated the same when it comes to SSA insurance benefits. The SSA has established a number of criteria that apply generally to widowed spouses and, in some cases, to divorced spouses of beneficiaries who die. Among the criteria a widowed spouse must meet is to be:

1. 60 years old or older.
2. disabled (following the criteria for disabled) and at least 50 years old but not yet 60 years old (you are entitled disabled widow(er)s benefits for Medicare coverage).
3. the spouse of a worker who was fully insured upon his or her death.
4. married to the deceased worker for at least the nine months just before the worker died.
5. the biological parent of the worker's child if a live child was born to you and the worker, even if the child did not survive.
6. the legally adopted parent of the worker's child. The adoption must have taken place during your marriage and the child must have been under age 18.
7. married to the worker when you both legally adopted a child who was then under age 18.
8. the spouse of a worker who legally adopted your child during your marriage and before the child reached age 18.

CLUE: You are *not* entitled to a spousal insurance benefit that is equal to or larger than the worker's primary insurance amount. However, if you were entitled to disability benefits under the Social Security Act, or an insurance annuity under the Railroad Retirement Act in the month *before* the month you married the deceased worker, you may be eligible for widow(er)'s (spousal) benefits. Those benefits may also not be larger than the worker's primary insurance amount.

DIVORCED SPOUSE: WHO GETS WHAT AND WHEN

If you were married to someone for ten years or longer before the divorce became final, you have reached the age requirement (62 or older), are not now married, and do not claim benefits on your own earnings, you may be able to claim benefits on your former spouse whether you are male or female.

HOW CAN I CLAIM BENEFITS ON MY DIVORCED SPOUSE'S EARNINGS?

Basically, to claim benefits on a divorced spouse's earnings, the rules for widow(er)s apply: You must be of retirement age and your spouse must have earned enough work credits to earn benfits. If your spouse is not eligible, you cannot receive benefits now but must wait until the eligibility is met. You must be 62 or older to collect benefits on a retired spouse, divorced or married, even if your minor or disabled children are entitled to benefits. Retirement or disability insurance benefits for a divorced spouse cannot equal or exceed one-half the worker's primary insurance amount.

A legally divorced spouse may be able to claim benefits on the former spouse's benefits if certain criteria are met:

1. An application must be filed for divorced spouse's benefits.
2. Your marriage must have lasted 10 years or longer.
3. You must be 62 or older.
4. If you are not entitled to retirement or disability insurance benefits, but you are 62 or older and fully insured yourself, you can become independently entitled to benefits on the worker's earnings record. You must meet the above requirements and be divorced from the worker for not less than two years in a row.

CAN THESE BENEFITS END?

When you marry or divorce, the month in which the marriage took place or the divorce was granted is a "nonmonth" in the eyes of the SSA. The rule is that a spouse is simply not entitled to a spouse's insurance benefits for the month in which they were married or remarried. Benefits will date from the month the SSA lists as the month you applied for and are eligible for the benefits.

When you, as the divorced spouse, are entitled to retirement or disability insurance benefits, and your primary insurance amount is at least one-half of the worker's primary insurance amount, you will be de-

SOCIAL SECURITY FOR THE CLUELESS

nied benefits *only* if you legally remarry someone other than the worker.

Benefits can end if the spouse learns that the marriage was invalid; the divorced spouse marries someone other than the worker; or for an independently entitled divorced spouse, the worker is no longer fully insured or he or she marries the worker. However, the spouse's benefit will not end by marrying an individual entitled to divorced spouse's, widow(er)'s, mother's, father's, or parent's monthly benefits, or to an individual age 18 or over who is entitled to childhood disability benefits.

When a spouse dies, his or her spousal benefits end. However, the surviving spouse may be able to receive survivors benefits. If you collect spousal benefits, they will be paid as long as you live but cannot be transferred when you die. If you do not collect spousal benefits and your spouse dies, you may collect survivors benefits if you qualify. Minor or disabled children are eligible for survivor benefits whenever a worker who has earned credits dies.

Should a worker's entitlement to disability insurance benefits end, and there are no retirement insurance benefits, your spousal benefits will also end. **EXCEPTION:** If the divorced spouse meets certain requirements, he or she may be eligible for his or her own benefits.

When the spouse is under age 62 and there are no children eligible for benefits, the spouse's benefits end.

WILL YOUR BENEFITS END IF YOU SAY "I DO" AGAIN?

If you want to remarry, you may be able to keep your benefits. The key is to remarry after you are 60 years old. You will retain your benefits on your deceased spouse's Social Security earnings record. If you remarry before you are 50, you will not be entitled to survivors benefits, unless the new marriage ends.

EXCEPTION: Remarriage as a disabled spouse allows you to retain benefits based on your deceased spouse's Social Security earnings records, as long as you were at least 50 years old when you remarried or if the remarriage occurred *after* you became disabled. If you remarry before you turn 60 and that subsequent marriage ends, you may become entitled or reentitled to benefits on your deceased spouse's earnings record. Your benefits begin the month the subsequent marriage ends. If the remarriage was annulled from the beginning you may not be eligible for benefits.

The following conditions must be met:

1. If your marriage is voided because of an illegality, your previous benefits may begin again as of the month the marriage ended.
2. If your marriage has been annulled by a court having jurisdiction over the matter, your benefits can be reinstated as of the month the decree of annulment was issued, if applied for in a timely fashion, usually within 60 days of the decree.
3. If your benefits ended because you remarried, other individuals may receive Social Security

benefits on the former spouse's earnings record, including:

a. a divorced spouse.
b. a parent.
c. a widow(er).
d. a surviving divorced spouse.
e. a surviving divorced parent.

5
CHILDREN AND SOCIAL SECURITY

BABY'S FIRST OFFICIAL IDENTITY— A SOCIAL SECURITY NUMBER

Getting your child a Social Security number is the first step to ensuring the benefits he or she will be eligible for in the future. Although applying for a Social Security card and number for your newborn is voluntary, it's a good idea to do it as soon as possible. It is a simple procedure, and many hospitals and birth registries provide the necessary papers on the spot. A Social Security number is necessary for any newborn whom you plan to claim as a dependent on your income tax return or a newborn for whom you will open a bank account, obtain government services, or buy savings bonds or medical coverage.

When you apply for a baby's Social Security number, the SSA will want to know the Social Security numbers for both parents, and then will issue a number for your child. Your child's Social Security card will be mailed to you within a few weeks.

If you prefer to wait until your child is a little older

to get an SSN, you can call the SSA at 800-772-1213, begin the application process online at www.ssa.gov/online/ss-5.html, or visit your local office. To expedite the procedure, bring the following with you:

1. a completed application form with both parents' Social Security numbers if both are claiming the child. Adults may opt to indicate single parenthood.
2. evidence of your child's age, identity, and citizenship, e.g., a birth certificate or birth registration form or, in some cases, a baptismal record
3. evidence of your identity as a parent or legal guardian

CLUE: The SSA never charges for a Social Security card and number. If you lose your own or your child's card, it will be replaced for free.

A child is defined as a person who is either an adopted or natural child and is eligible for benefits based on parents' work records. Stepchildren have some restrictions to claims on benefits of stepparents. They can receive Social Security benefits on a stepparent's earnings record only if the child depends on the stepparent for at least one-half of his or her financial support. If the stepparent was divorced from the child's parent after June 30, 1996, the stepchild is not eligible for benefits.

UNDERSTANDING
SOCIAL SECURITY NUMBERS

The first three digits are assigned by the region where the card was issued. People on the East Coast have lower numbers than the West Coast because the numbers began in the East and moved westward. The other six digits are randomly assigned. More than 400 million *different* numbers have been issued, and *none* is reused, although there may come a time when the billion possible combinations are used up.

HOW CHILDREN CAN BENEFIT FROM SOCIAL SECURITY AND SSI

A young working parent is a source of Social Security protection for the family. If either parent retires, dies, or becomes disabled and unable to work, the parent's earnings would be partially replaced by monthly Social Security benefits payments to the children.

Children can be eligible for benefits from either or both SSA and SSI (Supplemental Security Income) based on a number of factors, which include being:

- 18 years old or younger and part of an indigent family
- disabled
- survivors of a deceased working parent
- 19 years old and in elementary or high school full time

SOCIAL SECURITY BENEFITS FOR CHILDREN

Social Security dependents benefits are payable to children younger than 18, based on the record of a parent who is collecting retirement or disability benefits from Social Security. Survivors benefits are payable to children under the age of 18 on the record of a parent who has died. Survivors benefits can be paid on either a deceased mother's or a deceased father's work record.

When Children Reach Age 18

Your benefits as a child stop at age 18 unless you are a full-time student in an elementary or secondary school or you are disabled. Your earnings for the entire year in which you reach age 18 count in figuring the amount of benefits due you for the year, regardless of whether your payments continue or stop at age 18.

Adoption of a Child

Inform the SSA when you adopt a child. Information needed includes:

1. child's name
2. date of adoption decree
3. adopting parent's name and address
4. Social Security number of the child
5. Social Security number of birth parents, if known

When a Child Leaves the Care of a Wife, Husband, Widow, or Widower

If you are receiving benefits because you are caring for a child who is under 16 or who was disabled before he or she was 22, notify the SSA if the child leaves your care. Failure to report this could result in a penalty and loss of benefits.

A temporary separation may not affect your benefits as long as you still have parental control over the child.

> ### *CHANGES THAT ARE IMPORTANT TO REPORT*
>
> • **Change of address where you or the child lives.**
> • **If you no longer have responsibility for the child or if the child returns to your care.**
> • **If the child dies.**
> • **Your representative payee should inform the SSA if you die or become disabled.**

A Child Nearing Age 18 Who Is a Full-Time Student or Is Disabled

Payments to a child will stop when the child reaches 18 unless unmarried and either disabled or a full-time student at an elementary or secondary school.

Twice a year the SSA sends each student a form that should be filled out and returned. If the completed form is not returned, the student's payments will stop.

If a child 18 or older receives benefits as a student, the SSA should be notified immediately if the student:

- drops out of school
- changes schools
- changes from full-time to part-time attendance
- is expelled or suspended
- is paid by his or her employer for attending school
- marries
- begins working

The SSA can resume sending payments to the child if he or she becomes disabled before age 22 or is unmarried and enters elementary or secondary school on a full-time basis before age 19.

If a disabled child recovers from a disability and then is disabled again within seven years, benefits can be resumed.

MANAGING CHILDREN'S BENEFITS

Parents are usually empowered to manage the SS or SSI benefits sent to children. They should let the SSA know if they, or a representative payee will be handling the funds so that arrangements can be made by the SSA to send the payments to a relative or other person who can act on behalf of the child.

PARENTS CAN BE BENEFICIARIES
OF A CHILD

Although it is not common, some parents are supported by minor children. If a minor dies and the parent was dependent upon the child for more than half of his or her support, Social Security benefits may be provided if:

1. the parent is at least 62 years old and has not remarried since the minor worker's death.
2. the parent is not entitled to his or her own, higher Social Security benefit.
3. proof of support can be submitted to Social Security within two years of the minor worker's death.

Almost 4,000 parents age 62 or older are receiving monthly Social Security benefits on the record of a deceased child, and about 600,000 adults receive monthly benefits because they are a parent of a child receiving benefits from a working parent who is deceased.

Parents who qualify must have children in their care who are younger than 18; however, most benefits end on the sixteenth birthday of the child. The benefits to the child will continue until he or she reaches 18 or 19, provided the child remains in school full time.

SSA BENEFITS FOR DISABLED CHILDREN

Being a disabled child does not in itself qualify a child for Social Security benefits, because the SSA does not need to consider the disability to qualify a child for benefits. The SSA frequently pays for adults who were disabled as children and remain disabled into their twenties or thirties. The child must have a disability that began prior to his or her turning age 22.

SSI BENEFITS FOR CHILDREN

SSI is a program that pays monthly benefits to people with low incomes and limited assets who are 65 or older, or blind, or disabled. The purpose of Supplemental Security Income is not to replace, but to supplement, a person's income, and only up to a certain level. Above that level, the SSA would not consider them eligible. The level varies from one state to another because of many economic factors, and the level can go up every year based on cost-of-living (COLA) increases. Your local Social Security office can provide information on SSI benefit levels in your state.

QUALIFICATIONS FOR SSI

A child is qualified for SSI benefits based on his or her parent's income. Children may reside at home or be away from home at school if they return home occasionally and are the responsibility of their parents. This process is known as "deeming" income and assets.

For Children Eighteen and Older

The parent's income and assets are not considered as a basis for giving a child SSI benefits if that child is older than 18 because that child is now considered an adult. A child who was not eligible for SSI before his or her eighteenth birthday because the parent's income or assets were too high may become eligible at age 18 if he/she files independently of the family. Disabled children over 18 who continue to live with their parents but who cannot pay for food or shelter may be available for SSI.

Disabled Children Who Earn Benefits

If a child is disabled before age 22, he or she may receive a disability benefit. These benefits continue as long as they remain disabled and unable to work.

Criteria for Disability for SSI Benefits

The local Social Security office determines what children's income and assets fall within the SSI limits. However, determining what is a disability is usually done by the state, usually through its Disability Determination Service (DDS). The office team of a disability evaluation specialist, a medical doctor, and others will review each child's application to be designated disabled. In order to get complete information, the team may ask that the child undergo a special examination. *This service is free.* If the child does not undergo the examination or shows "poor effort," the DDS team may reject the application for disability benefits.

The law states that a child will be considered disabled if he or she has a physical or mental condition (or a combination of conditions) that results in "marked and severe functional limitations." The condition must last or be expected to last at least twelve months or be expected to result in the child's death.

The DDS evaluation specialist has a list of more than one hundred physical and mental symptoms or conditions, among which are: cerebral palsy, mental retardation, muscular dystrophy, and others, although a condition does *not* have to be on the list for the specialist to consider your case so long as the condition causes "marked and severe functional limitations." Teachers, counselors, therapists, social workers, doctors, and other health professionals who know or treat your child may be consulted.

A child must not be working at a job that the SSA considers "substantial work."

CLUE: The disability evaluation process generally takes several months, but the law includes special provisions for people signing up for SSI disability whose condition is so severe that they are presumed to be disabled. SSI benefits are paid for up to six months while the formal disability decision is being made. The conditions currently on the list are:

1. HIV infection
2. Down syndrome
3. significant mental deficiency
4. diabetes (with amputation of one foot)
5. amputation of two limbs
6. amputation of a leg at the hip
7. blindness

In some, but not all cases, SSI benefits will be made prior to the completion of the investigation for cerebral palsy, muscular dystrophy, and deafness.

The benefits do *not* have to be repaid if the DDS

avers the child's disability is not severe enough to qualify for ongoing SSI benefits.

Continuing Disability Reviews (CDR) are performed at least every three years for children under 18 whose conditions are expected to improve; and not later than twelve months after birth for babies whose disability is based on low birthweight. At the time of the reviews the parents, or representative payee, must present evidence that the child is and has been receiving medically necessary treatment.

Disability Reevaluations at Age 18

Under the law, children who are eligible for SSI benefits in the month before they turn 18 must have, in SSI vernacular, a redetermination—that is, their eligibility must be reevaluated. This is done during the one-year period beginning on the child's eighteenth birthday and follows the rules for adults filing new claims.

Children in Certain Medical Care Facilities

The monthly SSI payment will be limited to $30 (thirty dollars) for children under age 18 who live throughout a calendar month in certain institutions where private health insurance pays for their care.

Children with Disabilities and Adults Disabled Since Childhood

When a child who is getting dependents or survivors benefits from Social Security reaches 18, benefits stop unless the child is a full-time student in an elementary or high school and is up to and including 19 years old or is disabled and expected to remain disabled throughout his or her adult years.

EXCEPTION: Sam Smith begins receiving retirement benefits at age 62. His son Steve, who has had cerebral palsy since birth, is now eligible to collect a disabled "child's benefit" on his father's Social Security record even though Steve himself is no longer a minor.

To qualify for a child's disability benefit although an adult by age like Steve, the adult must have:

1. a physical or mental impairment.
2. a combination of impairments that are expected to prevent the adult child from doing any "substantial"* work for at least a year or that are expected to result in death.

The individual's condition is compared to a listing of impairments considered severe enough to prevent an individual from working for a year or more. If the individual is not working and has an impairment that meets or equals a condition on the list, then he or she is may qualify for disability benefits from Social Security. Every case is reviewed periodically to determine continuing eligibility.

*Generally, a job that pays $700 or more per month is considered "substantial."

HOW TO APPLY FOR YOUR CHILD'S BENEFITS FROM SOCIAL SECURITY OR SSI

You can call or visit your local Social Security office. Be prepared to show:

1. your child's Social Security number for either Social Security or SSI
2. your child's birth certificate for either Social Security or SSI
3. records of your income and your assets, and those of the child, for SSI
4. medical records for SSI (names, addresses, and telephone numbers of all doctors, hospitals, clinics, and others specialists treating your child or consulting on your child's case)
5. dates of visits to doctors or hospitals and account numbers for your child's medical records

Be prepared to discuss the day-to-day function or limits your child has and those he or she interacts with on a regular basis such as teachers, day-care providers, and family members. School records are a good source of information for the DDS.

WHEN BENEFITS STOP FOR MINORS

Your benefits as a child stop at age 18 unless you are a full-time student in an elementary or secondary school or you are disabled. Your earnings for the entire year in which you reach age 18 count in figuring the amount of benefits due you for the year, regardless of whether your payments continue or stop at age 18.

WHEN MEDICAID AND MEDICARE ARE APPLICABLE FOR CHILDREN'S BENEFITS

In many states, children who get SSI benefits also qualify for Medicaid. Some states offer Medicaid automatically, while others require that you sign up for these benefits. In some cases, a child who does not qualify for SSI may qualify for Medicaid. Your local Social Security office can answer questions about Medicaid coverage for your disabled child.

No child can get Medicare coverage until he or she is 20 years old.

EXCEPTION: Children with chronic renal disease who need a kidney transplant or maintenance dialysis can get Medicare if a parent is getting Social Security or has worked enough to be covered by Social Security.

OTHER HEALTHCARE SERVICES FOR CHILDREN

Federal and state governments have developed many helpful programs for families of disabled children and for the disabled child. These programs offer the emergency, day-to-day, and occasional medical therapy and treatment many disabled children need. Under the Children with Special Health Care Needs (CSHCN) provisions of the Social Security Act, these services are administered through state health agencies. The programs may be known as Children's Medical Services and Handicapped Children's Program.

Your United Way may also fund a variety of children's services directed at the medical treatment of disabled children. Many communities have hospitals that offer free care to children; they are usually named Shriner's Hospital or Children's Hospital and funded by charitable support groups. These hospitals offer extraordinary research and on-site care and treatment. Ask your medical practitioner, doctor, or therapist if your child is eligible for care at these facilities and to arrange a referral for you and your child.

MAJOR CLUE: Do not ever believe you or your disabled child is alone. Help is available at all levels of government. Ask your Social Security office for more information, or call your local United Way or Community Chest office.

READ MORE ABOUT SOCIAL SECURITY AND SSI BENEFITS FOR CHILDREN

Understanding the Benefits, Publication No. 05-10024
www.ssa.gov/pubs/10024
En Espanol, Publication No. 05-10924
www.ssa.gov/espanol/10924

Survivors Benefits, Publication No. 05-10084
www.ssa.gov/pubs/10084
En Espanol, Publication No. 05-10984
www.ssa.gov/espanol/10984

Disability Benefits, Publication No. 05-10029
www.ssa.gov/pubs/10029
En Espanol, Publication No. 05-10929
www.ssa.gov/espanol/10929

SSI, Publication No. 05-11000
www.ssa.gov/pubs/11000

CLUE: If you don't have a personal computer, many libraries, churches, and other nonprofit organizations provide Internet access services to the public. Call your local library for more information.

INFORMATION IS ALWAYS A PHONE CALL AWAY

You can get recorded information about Social Security and SSI twenty-four hours a day, including weekends and holidays, by calling 800-772-1213. You can speak to a service representative between the hours of 7 A.M. and 7 P.M. on business days. People who are deaf or hard of hearing may call the TTY number, 800-325-0778, between 7 A.M. and 7 P.M. on business days.

OTHER PUBLICATIONS OF INTEREST TO SURVIVORS

Retirement Benefits, Publication No. 05-10035— Explains Social Security retirement benefits.
Benefits for Children with Disabilities, Publication No. 05-10026—Explains benefits available to children with disabilities.

HOW TO FIND A LOCAL OFFICE

Social Security Administration
Office of Public Inquiries
6401 Security Boulevard
Room 4-C-5 Annex
Baltimore, MD 21235-6401
800-772-1213
or access www.ssa.gov/locator

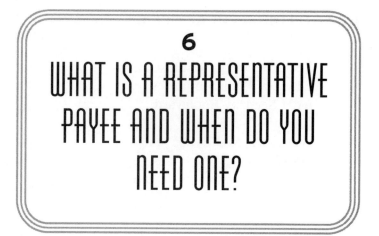

6
WHAT IS A REPRESENTATIVE PAYEE AND WHEN DO YOU NEED ONE?

MAJOR CLUE: Get an advocate *before* you need one. Most people will be able to take care of themselves and their financial affairs throughout their lives. However, illness, accident, and death can interfere with financial plans at any time. That's why, whether or not we want to think about such things, it is important to designate an advocate. Generally, a spouse, sibling, friend, or professional such as a lawyer or social worker is a good choice. The SSA refers to these advocates as representative payees.

Many people live alone by choice or circumstances. They are the ones who most need to keep the channels of communication open to an advocate, especially if they are elderly. A social worker, family member, or close friend can be a good choice for them, too.

Whether married, single and living with someone, single and living alone, or living in a community living center, you must designate someone to look after your affairs should you be unable to supervise them yourself. Consult your family or social worker *today* to determine who is the best choice at this time of your life. Review this choice yearly and change it if need be. Keep your advocate's name, telephone number, and other relevant information readily accessible near your telephone.

OTHER REASONS TO NAME A REPRESENTATIVE PAYEE

In this era of growing numbers of couples who live together but do not marry, one cannot assume that a partner has the same rights and privileges that a spouse does. If you live with someone, make sure they have power-of-attorney and other legal privileges to care for you in times of illness or to supervise your affairs at the time of death. The power-of-attorney designation is good for many purposes; however, the Social Security Administration does not accept it. Rather, it prefers working with a representative payee.

Accepting Representative Payee Responsibilities

This is an opportunity to make sure all your children have their own Social Security numbers (SSN), that yearly earnings statements have been sent to those who work, and that their records are up to date. You can also verify eligibility for Medicare, SSI, or other related programs that can help those friends or family members for whom you act as a representative payee.

WHEN A REPRESENTATIVE PAYEE IS AN ORGANIZATION OR INSTITUTION

Organizations or institutions that manage Social Security or SSI benefits for people in their institutions or under their care have similar responsibilities to that of individuals who act as representative payees. The primary goal of all is to manage the financial affairs, ensure that all food, shelter, and medical needs are met, and keep the Social Security office apprised of any changes. The primary difference between individuals and organizations/institutions is that organizations can collect a fee from the beneficiary check. To qualify, organizations or institutions must be:

- community based, nonprofit social service agencies, bonded or licensed in the state in which it serves as payee
- state or local government agencies with responsibility for income maintenance, social service, health care, or financial responsibilities
- regularly serving as a representative payee for at least five beneficiaries

The organization or institution cannot be a creditor of the beneficiaries, although some exceptions do apply. See your local office for explanations.

To collect a fee, organizations must request and obtain full authorizations from the local Social Security office. This authorization entitles them to be "Fees-for-Services" Representative Payees. They can collect monthly fees but CANNOT be reimbursed for any items considered overhead; the fee is to cover these "expenses."

WHO NEEDS A REPRESENTATIVE PAYEE?

Any beneficiary who becomes unable to manage their health care or/and their finances should seek the assistance of a Representative Payee or the SSA or SSI will appoint one for him or her. If an SSA or SSI beneficiary is in otherwise good health but chooses not to manage their finances themselves, they must accompany the Representative Payee when they perform financial arrangements for them, or prepare a written consent form so that the Representative Payee can handle their financial affairs. Most children under 18 years old have Representative Payees, usually their parents or guardians, and about 25 percent of all adults have payees for one reason or another.

DOES A REPRESENTATIVE PAYEE GET PAID?

Generally, no. An individual representative payee performs the services voluntarily and all payees are subject to the approval of the SSA. A representative payee can reimburse himself/herself for expenses incurred for the beneficiary such as for postage, money orders or checks for the beneficiary's bills, transportation for medical appointments, or other reasonable duties and items paid for on behalf of the beneficiary. Misuse of an SSA/SSI beneficiary's funds subjects the representative payee to a fine or imprisonment. All assistance provided by the Social Security Administration to either beneficiary or representative payee is always free.

HOW LONG DOES A REPRESENTATIVE PAYEE SERVE?

A representative payee may provide services until such time as the beneficiary recovers from a disability, decides to do without one and handle their own affairs, or if the beneficiary dies. In the case of children, the parent, legal guardian, or other interested party would probably serve until the child reaches 18 years of age or if another guardian, parent, or interested party is requested by the family.

A representative payee may not enter into binding contracts for a beneficiary but may do so if they are a parent or legal guardian, or if the adult beneficiary has granted the payee a proper power of attorney. Representative payees may acquire power-of-attorney rights as desired so by the beneficiary or by a financial institution, but mere power-of-attorney status is *not* acceptable to the SSA.

WHAT ARE THE RESPONSIBILITIES OF THE REPRESENTATIVE PAYEE?

The SSA views the responsibilities of the representative payee as more than financial management. He or she must ensure that day-to-day needs are met such as proper and sufficient food and shelter, clothing, and other ordinary expenses.

The representative payee must also manage expenses like hearing aids, eyeglasses, and dental care not provided by Medicare, Medicaid or, perhaps, the institution in which the beneficiary resides (nursing home, adult day care center, or similar). A minimum of $30 each month should be allowed for personal use by anyone in the institution, for such things as candy, toys, magazines or anything else that they desire; there are no restrictions on what is purchased.

And, of course, the representative payee must track SSA/SSI benefit receipts, pay bills, and account for anything left over from a beneficiary's benefits. That "leftover" is to be saved and maintained in a traditional financial institution like a savings and loan, credit union, or bank.

If the beneficiary has a dependent spouse, child, or parent living at the family home, part of the beneficiary's check may be used to support the legal dependent, provided that the current needs of the beneficiary are met first. If you have questions about providing monies to dependents, please ask your local Social Security office *before* making the expenditures.

If the beneficiary is a member of a family that receives Temporary Assistance for Needy Families (TANF) payments, those benefits may be used to support other family members, but it's always a good idea to verify with the SSA first before using funds for any other purpose, even if it is obviously used for the care and feeding of members of a household or family.

WHAT A REPRESENTATIVE PAYEE CANNOT DO

- sign any legal documents, except for those Social Security documents required on behalf of a beneficiary
- be a legal authority over earned income, pensions, or any income from sources other than Social Security or SSI

SOCIAL SECURITY FOR THE CLUELESS

- use a beneficiary's money for the payee's personal expenses, or spend funds in a way that would leave the beneficiary without necessary items or services (housing, food, medical care)
- put a beneficiary's Social Security or SSI funds in his or her own account or that of another person's
- use a beneficiary's "dedicated account" funds for basic living expenses (Note: This only applies to disabled/blind SSI beneficiaries under age 18.)
- keep conserved funds once you are no longer the payee
- charge the beneficiary for services unless authorized by SSA to do so. Usually, only organizations or institutions authorized as fee-for-service payees by the SSA may charge and collect fees.

"Current maintenance" is not limited to the usual institutional charges but includes expenditures, which aid the beneficiary's recovery or release from the institution to improve the beneficiary's condition while in the institution. This includes temporarily maintaining the beneficiary's home outside the institution unless a physician certifies that the beneficiary is unlikely to return home.

WHAT DOES AN SSI REPRESENTATIVE PAYEE DO?

Representative payees receiving SSI payments for a child (under 18 years of age) may be required to get proper treatment for the child's disabling condition when necessary. Failure to obtain medical treatment is just cause for the SSA to remove a person from serving as a representative payee. When in doubt, contact your local Social Security office.

WHAT IF THE BENEFICIARY GETS A WINDFALL?

If the beneficiary receives a large sum of money from an inheritance, a gift, a bonus from previous work, even winning the lottery, or, as in some cases, a large sum of money from the SSA, the representative payee must manage this extra windfall of money. He or she may spend it on anything that would improve the daily living conditions of the beneficiary, from better medical care to better housing, or, as appropriate, training to make him or her more self-sufficient.

Major health-related expenses can also be paid for when the beneficiary has received large sums of money. Among these possible expenses could be reconstructive dental care, a motorized wheelchair, rehabilitation expenses or insurance premiums, special training programs, or school tuition or daily school expenses. It can also be used for recreation—movies, concerts, magazine subscriptions, or special trips. Again, the objective of all monies handled by a representative payee are to enhance the life of the beneficiary.

Larger purchases that are acceptable may include anything from a down payment on a home to home improvements that make the home more accessible like a chair lift, wheelchair ramp, widened doorways, and any needed repairs from wear and tear. Furniture or appliances, especially those that can be shared with other household members, are also appropriate. And, a car or van may be purchased if used for and owned by the beneficiary for his or her personal transportation. Any questions you may have about expenditures should be addressed to the SSA before you pay them. Otherwise, the SSA may dismiss you as the representative payee.

CLUE: SSA beneficiaries may have extra resources. The limit for SSI resources is $2,000. Not all sources are counted towards the $2,000 limit, but a computer, expensive jewelry, or an elaborate sound system most likely will make an SSI beneficiary ineligible for future payments. Always check with the SSA before making a major purchase.

THE DEDICATED ACCOUNT AND WHO NEEDS TO USE IT

Some blind/disabled children may receive large past-due SSI payments covering more than six months of benefits. These payments must be paid directly into a separate account called a "dedicated account," because the funds can only be used for expenses directly related to the child's disability. These include:

- personal needs assistance
- special equipment
- housing modification
- therapy or rehabilitation
- medical treatment
- education or job skills training

- any other item or service related to the child's disability

When in doubt about whether something is appropriate to be bought, contact your Social Security office to make sure the product or service is on the allowable list.

Any money from the dedicated account spent for anything other than the expenses shown above, must be repaid to the Social Security Administration from your own funds. Be sure to keep a meticulous record of all money used from the dedicated account, including receipts for all products and services purchased as they are subject to review by the SSA.

No other funds may be commingled into a dedicated account, and money in the dedicated account does not count as an SSI resource. Interest earned on the money in a dedicated account also does not count as income or a resource.

Money for dedicated accounts or regular accounts for the beneficiary may be received by direct deposit so as not to be commingled with the personal accounts of the representative payee. Anything left over must be saved in U.S. savings bonds or in an interest-paying bank account, insured under federal or state law. Interest paid on savings belongs to the beneficiary. The beneficiary must be shown as the only owner of all accounts, under such titles as "(beneficiary's name) by (your name), representative payee," or "(your name), representative payee for (beneficiary's name)." Ask your bank to verify if there are any other acceptable ways to handle the naming of these accounts.

Although parents may have a common checking

account for all family members who receive benefits, the parent should be shown as the owner of the account. Savings for each child must be held in a savings account that shows the child's name as the *sole* owner of the account even if they are under 18 years old.

DOES THE SSA HAVE FORMS TO TRACK FINANCES?

Absolutely! To keep track of funds, use a Representative Payee Report (Form SSA-623, SSA-6230, or SSA-6233). Parents, grandparents, and stepparents who are payees for children in their custody should use Form SSA-6230. Payees of beneficiaries with dedicated accounts should use Form SSA-6233. The SSA will mail the appropriate form to you each year that you serve as a representative payee. You must complete the accounting form even if you are a legal guardian; the accounting you make to the court cannot be substituted.

Please see the next page for an SSA-approved worksheet to help you track expenditures for the beneficiary under your care. Use the data from this worksheet to complete the representative payee report each year. Call the Social Security for another copy of the worksheet or download it from the Internet (www.ssa.gov/payee/organizations/ExhibitE.pdf) and print it out.

Social Security will mail you a Social Security Benefit Statement (Form SSA-1099) that shows the amount of benefits paid during the previous year. This should be given to the beneficiary's tax preparer in case any benefits are subject to taxes.

Income and Expense Worksheet

Month and Year	Amount of payments received	Expenses for food and housing	Expenses for clothing, medical/dental, personal items, recreation, miscellaneous
Totals for Report period	$ —————	$ ————— Put this figure on line 3B of the Representative Payee Report	$ ————— Put this figure on line 3C of the Representative Payee Report

Show the total amount of any benefits you saved including any interest earned. $ ————————

Put this figure on line 3D of the Representative Payee Report.

Directions:

1. This form is optional. You are free to design your own form or use another record-keeping method.

2. Make copies of this form before you use it so you will always have blank copies.

WHAT IS A COLLECTIVE ACCOUNT AND WHO CAN USE IT?

Sometimes nursing homes or other institutions place funds for several beneficiaries in a single checking or savings account. This is called a "collective account." This is usually acceptable, but special rules apply to these accounts. You are required to set aside a minimum of $30 per person each month to be used for the beneficiary's personal needs or saved on his or her behalf (for candy, magazines, or what have you. This amounts to one dollar a day, but it helps return dignity and some sense of control to even the most indigent or incapacitated of beneficiaries).

Examples of collective account titles include: "The Golden Years Nursing Home, Representative Payee for Social Security beneficiaries" or "The Golden Years Patients' Fund for Social Security beneficiaries."

If your institution is serving as a payee and considering charging the beneficiary for past care and maintenance costs, they will need to get prior approval from your local Social Security office. SSA also needs to approve any decision to pool the personal funds of several beneficiaries to purchase an item that will benefit the group.

CLUE: If Medicaid is paying more than half the cost of an SSI beneficiary's care or private health insurance is paying for a child's care, the SSI payment is usually limited to $30 per month plus any additional money paid by the state. This entire payment must be used for the beneficiary's personal needs or be saved on his or her behalf.

WHAT CHANGES TO REPORT AND WHEN

A representative payee needs to tell Social Security about any changes that may affect the checks you receive. As payee, you are liable for repayment of money you received on behalf of the beneficiary if any of the events listed below occur and you do not report them. For example, report if the beneficiary: dies; moves; starts or stops working, no matter how small the amount of earnings is; begins receiving another government benefit, or the amount of the benefit changes; will be outside the United States for thirty days or more; is incarcerated for a crime that carries a sentence of over one month; is committed to an institution by court order for a crime committed because of a mental impairment; marries or divorces; or no longer needs a payee.

Also, inform the SSA if the beneficiary is disabled and his or her condition improves. If the beneficiary is a child, inform the SSA if the child is adopted, is no longer in the custody of the parent or legal guardian on record, or if the child's parents divorce or die. If the child is a stepchild, inform the SSA if the parents divorce.

WHAT SHOULD THE REPRESENTATIVE PAYEE DO FOR SSI BENEFICIARIES?

Generally, when there are major changes to the life of a beneficiary, those changes must be reported to the SSI. For example, if the beneficiary moves from a home, hospital, nursing home, or other institution; marries or divorces (or spouse dies); changes the status of the household by allowing someone to move in or out; or has resources that change. A child's SSI check may change if there are any changes in the family's income or resources.

CLUE: If you are a representative payee for a person who receives SSI benefits, be aware that all resources, including savings, are limited to $2,000, including the interest that is earned on any savings accounts. A child's dedicated savings account, however, does not count toward the $2,000 limit.

REPRESENTATIVE PAYEE AND MEDICARE/MEDICAID

A representative payee may need to help the beneficiary obtain medical services or treatment. Always have at the ready the Medicare card or State Medicaid Eligibility Card of the beneficiary; it will be shown to the person or place providing the medical service. Keep a record of medical services the beneficiary receives and medical expenses not covered by Medicare and Medicaid. This is especially important if the beneficiary is a blind or disabled child. For information about Medicare coverage, call Social Security to ask for a copy of *The Medicare Handbook* (HCFA Publication No. 10050).

If the beneficiary has low income and few resources, the state may pay Medicare premiums and some out-of-pocket medical expenses. A person may qualify even if his or her income or resources are too high for SSI. For more information, contact the state or local medical assistance (Medicaid) agency, social service office, or welfare office.

WHAT IF YOU STOP BEING THE REPRESENTATIVE PAYEE?

If you will no longer be the payee, you must notify Social Security immediately. This is important because a new payee will have to be selected as soon as possible.

When you are no longer responsible for the beneficiary, you must return any benefits, including interest and cash on hand to the Social Security Administration. The funds will then be reissued to the beneficiary or to the new payee. In some cases, you will be asked to turn over refunds to the beneficiary or to the new payee.

WHAT IF A BENEFICIARY BELIEVES A REPRESENTATIVE PAYEE IS NO LONGER NECESSARY?

When a beneficiary obtains the services of a representative payee because of his or her physical or mental disability, the only way to dismiss the payee is to prove that he is currently able mentally and physically to handle his financial affairs by himself. To do this, the beneficiary must provide the SSA with the following:

- a doctor's statement that, due to change or improvement in your condition, he or she believes you are now capable of self-care
- a court order stating that the court believes you are now capable of self-care
- other demonstrable evidence that shows an ability for self-care

MAJOR CLUE ALERT!! If your condition has improved to the point that the SSA now believes you no longer need a representative payee, they may reevaluate your eligibility for benefits. This is particularly true of SSI recipients.

You, as a beneficiary, also have the right to appeal either the decision that you need a representative payee, or the person or organization SSA has chosen as your representative payee. You have sixty days to appeal a decision by contacting SSA. Please contact your local Social Security office or call 800-772-1213 for more information.

CLUE: If you believe that the representative payee is not working on your behalf or is acting illegally or unethically, contact the SSA immediately. You will be appointed a substitute payee. If you have been dismissed as a representative payee, and feel that dismissal is unwarranted, you have the right to appeal this decision within sixty days. See page 180 for an explanation of the Appeals Process.

WHAT SHOULD YOU DO IF THE BENEFICIARY DIES?

If the beneficiary dies, saved benefits belong to his or her estate. They must be given to the legal representative of the estate or otherwise handled according to state law. If you need information about state law, contact the probate court or an attorney.

When a person who receives Social Security dies, no check is payable for the month of death, even if he or she dies on the last day of the month. Any check received for the month of death or later must be returned.

An SSI check, however, is payable for the month of death. But you must return any SSI checks that come after the month of death.

RECEIVING SSI FOR CHILDREN

Representative payees receiving SSI payments for a child (under 18 years of age) may be required to get proper treatment for the child's disabling condition when necessary. When in doubt, contact your local Social Security office. Failure to obtain medical treatment is just cause for the SSA to remove you from the position as representative payee. The rules that govern being a representative payee for a child are the same as those for being a representative payee for an adult. (See pages 68–75.)

FOR MORE INFORMATION

You can get recorded information twenty-four hours a day, including weekends and holidays, by calling Social Security's toll-free number, 800-772-1213. You can speak to a service representative between the hours of 7 A.M. and 7 P.M. on business days. The lines are busiest early in the week and early in the month, so if your business can wait, it's best to call at other times. If you'd like general information about Social Security and SSI benefits, ask for a copy of the booklet *Understanding the Benefits* (Publication No. 05-10024).

People who are deaf or hard of hearing may call the

toll-free TTY number, 800-325-0778, between 7 A.M. and 7 P.M. on business days or access www.ssa.gov.

PUBLICATIONS OF INTEREST TO REPRESENTATIVE PAYEES

For information about Medicare coverage, read *The Medicare Handbook* (HCFA Publication No. 10050) or access www.ssa.gov/pubs/10050. En Espanol, HCFA Publication No. 10950 or access www.ssa.gov/espanol/10950.

For more information about SSI read *What You Need To Know When You Get SSI* (Publication No. 05-11011) or access www.ssa.gov/pubs/11101. En Espanol, Publication No. 05-11911 or access www.ssa.gov/espanol/11911.

People who are deaf or hard of hearing may call the toll-free TTY number, 800-325-0778, between 7 A.M. and 7 P.M. on business days.

All of these publications are available at any local Social Security office or access them at www.ssa.gov.

DISABILITY BENEFITS REQUIRE EARNED CREDITS, TOO

Payments for disability benefits are determined in the same way that retirement benefits are. You pay into a fund with each paycheck and earn credits based on your overall work earnings. The younger you are, the fewer credits you will need because you will have had fewer years in which to earn credits. Conversely, the older you are, the more credits you will need, and the same number of credits (40) is needed for retirement age of 62 or older.

The age and credit ratio if you become disabled, is as follows:

Age 24 or younger: 6 credits during the three-year period ending when your disability began.

Age 24 through 30: credits for half the period between 21 and the age and time you become disabled.

Age 31 or older: credits as noted below. Twenty of these credits must have been earned in the ten years immediately before you became disabled.

Age 62 or older: 40 credits.

DISABLED AT AGE	CREDITS NEEDED
31 through 42	20
44	22
46	24
48	26
50	28
52	30
54	32
56	34
58	36
60	38
62 or older	40

SURVIVORS BENEFITS WHEN CREDITS ARE FEWER THAN 40

The family of a deceased worker may receive survivors benefits, even though the deceased did not earn enough credits for his or her own retirement benefits.

For dependent children of a deceased worker, it does not matter when the worker was born; it matters how old the children are. Dependent children may receive survivors benefits if the deceased worker had 6 credits in the three years before his or her death. The dependent children can receive benefits until they are 18 years old, or until age 19 if they are attending elementary or secondary school full-time.

If the deceased worker was born in 1929 or before, 1 credit is needed for each year after 1950 and prior to the year of death, up to a maximum of 40 credits, for family members to collect survivors benefits.

If the deceased worker was born in 1930 or later, 1 credit is needed for each year after age 21 and prior to the year of death, up to a maximum of 40 credits.

A widow or widower caring for dependent children who are under 16 years old or are disabled also may be able to get benefits. For more information, read the booklet *Understanding the Benefits* (Publication No. 05-10024) or access www.ssa.gov/pubs/10024.

SOME WORKERS DO NOT EARN CREDITS

Not all employees work in jobs covered by Social Security and Medicare, including, ironically, many federal employees hired before 1984. However as of January 1, 1983, all federal employees have paid the Medicare hospital insurance part of the Social Security tax and all are now covered.

Other employees who have not earned Social Security credits include railroad employees with more than ten years of service; employees of some state and local governments that chose not to participate in

Social Security; and children under age 21 who work for a parent such as on a family farm (different from a child age 18 or older who works in the parent's business).

MEDICARE

The credits you earn from your work also count toward your eligibility for Medicare, the hospital and health care program available when you reach age 65. People who need kidney dialysis or a kidney transplant for permanent kidney failure may be eligible for Medicare at any age. You may also be eligible for Medicare if you are disabled for twenty-four months or more, and your dependents or survivors may be eligible for Medicare when they are age 65 or if they are disabled.

For more information, read the publication *Medicare & You*, Publication No. HCFA 05-10050 or access www.medicare.gov.

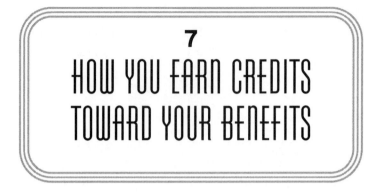

7
HOW YOU EARN CREDITS TOWARD YOUR BENEFITS

You earn Social Security credits when you work in a job where the employer and you pay Social Security taxes (FICA). The credits are based on your earnings and the number required (40 or more) depends upon the year in which you were born. Many older Americans, especially those born before 1929, need fewer credits because Social Security only began in 1935. Most people born after 1929 require 40 or more credits to earn benefits. The following chart details the specifics:

YEAR OF BIRTH	CREDITS NEEDED
1929 or later	40
1928	39
1927	38
1926	37
1925	36
1924	35

All credits remain on your record whether or not you work in any particular year. They can always be added to, depending upon your job and the earnings from it.

Each year the amount of earnings needed for a credit rises as average earnings levels rise. In 2001, for example, 1 credit was awarded for each $830 of earnings, up to the maximum of 4 credits per year.

IF YOU ARE SELF-EMPLOYED

You can earn Social Security credits the same way employees do (1 credit for each $830 in net earnings, but no more than 4 credits per year). However, because you have no employer to share the burden of taxation, you pay all of your Social Security tax obligations, about 15 percent of your earnings. If your work earns you less than $400 per year, there are exceptions to the rules. For more information online, go to the Web site at www.ssa.gov/pubs/10022.html, and read the fact sheet *If You're Self-Employed,* Publication No. 05-10022.

IF YOU'RE IN THE MILITARY

You can now earn Social Security credits the same way employees in the private sector do, and you may even receive additional earnings credits under certain conditions. For more information online, go to the Web site at www.ssa.gov/pubs/10017.html, and read the fact sheet *Military Service and Social Security,* Publication No. 05-10017.

OTHER EXCEPTIONS

If you provide domestic work as a maid or house-keeper, if you are a farm worker, or if you work for a church, other rules may apply. Churches, and most religious organizations, are often exempted from paying Social Security taxes. If you are a church employee, clergy, or layman and do not pay into the FICA (Social Security account), you may be required to pay at the same rate as a "self-employed" person even though you are an employee. When your employer has exempt status this puts an increased tax burden on you, in many cases.

For more information, call 800-772-1213, from 7 A.M. to 7 P.M. on any business day. The deaf or hard of hearing may call the TTY number, 800-325-0778, 7 A.M. to 7 P.M. on any business day. Or access www.ssa.gov

IF YOU CONTINUE TO WORK WHILE RECEIVING SOCIAL SECURITY BENEFITS

Many people choose to continue to work even though they are old enough to retire and may opt not to collect their SSA benefits, and others, often for economic reasons, continue to work while receiving SSA benefits. Minimum retirement age is 62, and anyone who is age 62 through 69 who works and collects benefits can earn only a limited amount without losing some of the benefits from Social Security. (After age 70, earnings don't count against your benefits.)

These losses can be considerable (more than 20 percent), so when you apply for benefits, the SSA will inform you what the limits are at that time and whether earnings (from a job or a business) will affect your monthly benefits. This is particularly important for anyone who files for benefits at age 62 or less than full retirement age. Not only will they will receive a lower amount of benefits than if they waited until full retirement age, but this lower rate can practically disappear if they earn a substantial income during the period when they are 62 to 69 years old.

Because of today's longer life expectancies, the full retirement age will gradually increase until 2003, when it will reach age 67, affecting people born in 1938 and later.

When choosing when to begin receiving benefits, you should consider a number of factors: your possible lifespan, the amount of your other income, whether your income is so low that it is necessary to collect your benefits when you're first eligible, or whether it will be more beneficial to work until age 70. The SSA encourages later retirement and frequently provides a "bonus" for those who retire at age 70 or older.

Your accountant or a Social Security representative can assist you in this very vital decision-making process, or you can read the booklet *Retirement Benefits*, Publication No. 05-10035; go to the retirement benefits keyword at www.ssa.gov/pubs/ 10035.html; or see page 98 for a fuller explanation.

> *[The purpose of government is] to do for a community of people whatever they need to have done but cannot do at all or cannot do so well for themselves in their separate and individual capacities.*
>
> —Abraham Lincoln

8
HOW TO APPLY
FOR BENEFITS

Applying for benefits can be just a phone call away. The first thing to do is call the toll-free number, 800-772-1213, and ask whether you can receive either retirement or survivors benefits with this one phone call. As always, have ready your basic information (see below). If it's not possible to complete the process by phone, you can visit the SSA office or begin the process online.

CLUE: The point is to start the process as soon as you are eligible; loss of time could mean a delay in receiving benefits.

HERE'S HOW IT WORKS

You may use the SSA Web site to apply for Social Security benefits, but as for all applications online, it is only the beginning. You can obtain and fill out an application form online, but remember that you must still deliver the application to a local office or mail it *with original documents*. All the requested documents will be returned. See below for more details.

Access www.ssa.gov and click on "Forms." You will be linked up to an official form. Then:

1. Enter the information requested.
2. Send your information to the SSA, as requested, over the Internet.
3. Print out the application and sign it.
4. Gather all the required documents and send them along with the signed *paper* application to your local Social Security office, or bring them in with you when you visit.

Online applications are accepted (Eastern Time) 6 A.M. to 1 A.M., Monday through Friday, 8 A.M. to 11 P.M. on Saturday, 8 A.M. to 8 P.M. on Sunday.

WHAT IS THE PURPOSE OF THE APPLICATION? AREN'T BENEFITS GUARANTEED?

The application is the source of information that Social Security uses to determine whether or not you, your spouse, and/or your children are eligible for benefits. Before you fill on an application, be prepared to give the following information:

1. Social Security number
2. date and place of birth
3. bank or financial institution's Routing Transit Number and your bank account number so your benefits can be deposited electronically into your account. The routing number identifies the bank to Social Security. It is the nine-digit number at the bottom left of your check. It may also ap-

pear on your checking account bank statement or on your personal checking account deposit slip. It is the financial institutions, not you, who make the arrangements for direct deposit with the SSA.

Earnings are important information to determine benefits. Be prepared to list what you earned last year, how much you expect to earn this year, and possibly how much you expect to earn the year after that. Partial year amounts, such as earnings between September and December, may be requested.

Where you earned the money is important, too. Be prepared to give the business name and address of any and all employers during the last three years. If you were self-employed, state that information.

Anyone who served in any branch of the U.S. military (Army, Navy, Air Force, Marines, National Guard, Coast Guard), Public Health Service (PHS), or Coast & Geodetic Survey (CGS) should be prepared to give the starting and ending dates of the service period. To expedite this, have your original discharge papers with you.

Be prepared to give the name, Social Security number, and date of birth of your current and/or any prior spouse to whom you were legally married; the date and place of each marriage; and if appropriate, the date and place of any divorce. Proof of any annulment may be requested. Ask Social Security if it is necessary.

The SSA sends a Social Security Statement every year to all Americans over the age of 25, usually three months prior to your birth date. This has been done only since 1999, so examine it carefully to make sure that earnings are listed accurately. U.S. military service and work years after 1977 have the most errors, so be extra careful in your review. Do not, however, wait until the earnings record is corrected; send it along with your corrections or a letter stating the facts, because delaying this information could delay your benefits. If you do not have a statement, the SSA will send you one. Just call 800-772-1213.

As with most applications, to apply for Social Security benefits requires *original* documents of the following:

1. birth certificate or other proof of birth
2. naturalization papers, as applicable
3. U.S. military discharge paper(s), as applicable
4. W-2 Form(s) and/or self-employment tax returns for last year

CLUE: This is the only document Social Security will accept as copies. All others must be original, to protect you from unauthorized use or fraud.

THE YEAR SSA BENEFITS START

In figuring your total earnings for the year you first become entitled to benefits, count earnings in that year for months both before and after you become entitled.

HOW MUCH WILL YOUR BENEFITS BE WHEN YOU RETIRE?

Find out today with a free *Personal Earnings and Benefit Estimate Statement*. In it you'll find all your earnings listed, and the estimated retirement benefits you will earn at minimum and maximum retirement age. Call Social Security's toll-free number, 800-772-1213, and ask for Form SSA-7004.

If you are under full retirement age, $1 in benefits will be withheld for each $2 in earnings above the limit.

You must count your earnings for the whole year in figuring the benefits due you, generally earnings from the calendar year of January through December.

People who are full retirement age or older do not have an earnings limit.

THE YEAR SSA BENEFITS START

In figuring your total earnings for the year you first become entitled to benefits, the SSA will count earnings in that year for months both before and after you became entitled.

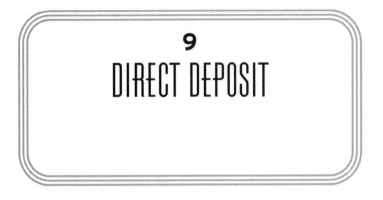

9
DIRECT DEPOSIT

Direct deposit is the safest way to receive your Social Security or Supplemental Security Income benefit checks. The checks, which come from the U.S. Treasury, are sent via electronic message to your personal account at a bank, savings and loan institution, or credit union. You can use these funds just as you would any others deposited into your account. You can withdraw money, put some in savings accounts, and write checks. Direct deposit is secure, is safe, and arrives in a timely manner. You can, however, still receive your benefits by mail, and you can change your decision at any time.

All you need to do is ask the direct deposit representative at your financial institution (savings and loan, bank, or credit union) to arrange the transaction for you. Just take your bank statement or personal check with you to show them your account number, and have your Social Security card available so that they can copy your number.

CLUE: A direct deposit sign up-form can be downloaded from http://www.ssa.gov/deposit/1199a. pdf.

Some individuals prefer not to have a checking account; however, they will still be able to receive their benefit checks electronically through a new low-cost account called the ETA (Electronic Transfer Account). To activate an ETA account, call the SSA toll-free number, 800-772-1213. They will need to have a bank account number (for a savings account or holiday account) and their Social Security number.

You should allow thirty to sixty days to activate this procedure, so it's a good idea to do this at the same time you register for your benefits. You will get a letter informing you of the date to expect the check to arrive. Your check will arrive in your account the same time each month; however, you can always call the bank to verify this.

If a representative payee is handling your financial affairs, he or she can have your benefit check directly deposited into another account to draw upon for your expenses and other needs.

Direct deposit saves you worry about lost or stolen checks and it saves the government about 40 cents per check. The typical costs to process and mail a check is 42 cents; to send it electronically costs only 2 cents! If all beneficiaries used direct deposit, it would save the government $8.4 million per *month*.

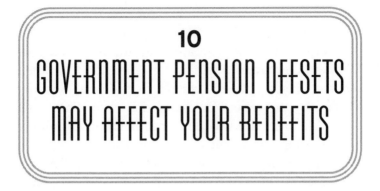

10
GOVERNMENT PENSION OFFSETS MAY AFFECT YOUR BENEFITS

In years past, spousal benefits remained unchanged even though the wage earner or his or her spouse earned a Civil Service pension. That has changed. Today, some government pensions offset (or reduce) Social Security benefits by two-thirds, a substantial amount.

When the Social Security program began, some government agencies did not contribute taxes to the program because they provided separate pensions for their employees. If you, or your spouse, worked for a federal, state, or local government that didn't pay FICA taxes, then it is likely that you or your beneficiaries will have reduced Social Security benefits.

A spouse or widow(er) who receives a government pension may not be eligible for Social Security benefits on a spouse's record. Some, or all, of spousal or widow(er) benefits may be offset (or reduced) by the pension from any job where Social Security taxes were not paid. For example, if you receive a Civil Service pension of $900, then $600, or two-thirds, will be offset or subtracted from your Social Security spouse's or widow(er)'s benefits. If you are eligible for a $700

Social Security widow(er)'s benefit, you'll receive only $100 per month ($700 - $600 = $100).

Before the offset provisions became law, many government employees qualified for a pension from their agency plus a spouse's benefit from Social Security earned by the retired or disabled spouse. They were then able to receive two pensions: their own from their own earnings, and their spousal benefit.

For example, John Jones collects a Social Security retirement benefit of $900 per month. His wife, June, is potentially eligible for a spousal benefit of up to 50 percent of John's benefits, or $450. If June worked at a job where she paid into Social Security, she also qualifies for her own retirement benefits.

CLUE: Here's where the change comes in: June can no longer, by law, receive the spousal benefit check of $450 plus her individual benefit check of $750. Instead, she is entitled to only one check. Obviously, she should choose the higher of the two SSA benefits for which she is eligible. In this scenario, her own individual benefit of $750 is higher than her spousal benefit of $450. This is an interpretation of one benefit amount "offsetting" another.

In another example, Tim Thompson also earns a $900 Social Security benefit check each month but his wife Tina worked not in the private sector but for the federal government, from which she earned a Civil Service pension of $700. Previously Tina could have received both her Civil Service pension ($700) and her spousal pension on Tim's record (50 percent of $900 or $450).

Today, with the offset provision, she does not qualify for the spousal benefit and can receive only her Civil Service pension of $700. Both women in these examples are spouses and both worked, but Tina is not eligible for her Civil Service pension and her spousal SSA benefit, only her pension, and June is not eligible for both her SSA benefit and her spousal benefit; she must choose only one. (Nobody said life was fair.)

Some government agencies remain exempt from offset subtractions. For example, any military service employee whose government pension is based on a job where he or she was paying Social Security taxes on the *last* day of employment, not necessarily over a long period of time, avoids the offset rule.

Individuals whose government pensions are not based on earnings are exempt. Others are exempt because many of these rulings or laws about offsetting pensions occurred long after they were eligible for pensions.

For example, individuals who received or were eligible to receive government pensions *before* December 1982 are exempt. Individuals who otherwise meet all the requirements for spousal benefits from Social Security that were in effect January 1977 are also exempt. Individuals who received or were eligible to receive a federal, state, or local government pension before July 1, 1983, and received one-half of their support from their spouse are also exempt.

Civil Service offset employees are those federal employees who were rehired after December 31, 1983, following a break in service of more than 365 days and who had five years of prior Civil Service Retirement

System [CSRS] employment. Any federal employees, including Civil Service Offset employees, who are required to participate in Social Security are exempt.

Federal employees who chose to switch from CSRS to the Federal Employees' Retirement System (FERS) on or before December 31, 1987, and those employees who were allowed to make a belated switch to FERS through June 30, 1988, may be exempt. Employees who switched programs beyond these time periods, including the time between July 1, 1998, and December 31, 1998, need five years under FERS to be exempt from the government pension offset.

CLUE: If you are or were a CRSE or FERS employee, check with your agency's pension or personnel department for more information. It is another way to check and double-check that you will get all the benefits earned. Don't depend on others to ensure the accuracy of your own records.

CLUE: Medicare is unaffected by offsetting. Medicare is available to everyone upon reaching age 65, regardless of whether or not they have a pension, receive a spousal SSA benefit, or earn an SSA benefit from their own work record.

CLUE: The offset applies only to Social Security benefits as a spouse or widow(er). However, your own benefits may be reduced owing to another provision of the law. Contact Social Security for the factsheet *A Pension From Work Not Covered by Social Security,* Publication No. 05-10045, or access www. ssa.gov/pubs/ 10045.html.

Offset pensions are governed by many rules and regulations. These pensions are particularly complicated and involve a great many exceptions, and some of them subject to change at any time. For more information, call 800-772-1213. If you are deaf or hard of hearing, call the TTY number, 800-325-0778, between 7 A.M. and 7 P.M. on business days, or read the factsheet *Government Pension Offset*, Publication No. 05-10007. You can also access it at www.ssa.gov/pubs/ 10007.html. For information in Spanish, get *En Español:* Publication No. 05-10907, or access www.ssa.gov/ pubs/10907.html.

11
LIVING ABROAD AND SOCIAL SECURITY

The SSA has developed a complete program to meet the needs of all workers and their dependents who receive Social Security benefits, and who live and/or work outside the United States. Whether it's retirement, long-term traveling, or working overseas that takes you away from the United States, if you or your family members receive Social Security benefits here, you can often arrange to receive your payments abroad.

You can opt to continue the direct deposit option to your U.S. financial institution or have your benefits checks deposited into a foreign financial institution. A third option is to keep the money here in the United States and empower a representative payee to send money to you as needed.

Most of the restrictions about receiving benefits stateside also apply to receiving them abroad. You must keep the SSA informed about any changes to marital status or disability. Upon your death, your beneficiaries must inform the SSA immediately to avoid SSA overpayments and penalties.

Whether or not you are collecting Social Security

benefits, obligations for taxes follow you whenever you choose to live abroad, especially if you are earning money from a business, a job, or even an apprenticeship in a foreign country.

CLUE: Don't fudge. The SSA always figures it out; you'll be subject to fines, or even jail, if you do not report your earnings accurately and in a timely fashion. If, for any reason, your traveling or living outside the country makes it difficult to communicate with the SSA, request that your representative payee do the reporting at the necessary time.

If you are traveling or visiting a country for a fairly short time, say, three months or less, you can probably just have your benefits deposited directly into your regular checking account. It may not be worth the paperwork to have them sent abroad. If you choose to go around the world on a dream trip for a year, going from country to country, it is definitely best to have all your Social Security checks go to one place. If that place is your hometown financial institution, your representative payee can always check that each month's benefit check has indeed arrived, and have the bank make transfers, as necessary, to wherever you are whenever you need more funds. If instead, you want the payments to be sent to your home base abroad, choose a country and a financial institution which accepts direct deposit from the U.S. (listed on page 109).

If you choose to live abroad permanently, or at least for several years, then making arrangements for a direct deposit to a bank near where you plan to live is the best idea, especially if your benefits are a primary part of your income.

Assistance for U.S. citizens visiting or living abroad is as close as the nearest U.S. embassy or consulate. The only catch is that some countries do not have relations or treaties with the United States, so please read through this chapter carefully to determine if the countries you'll be visiting or living in have arrangements with the United States to receive your check at their financial institutions.

We are so used to the speed and efficacy of banking, including direct deposit, here in the States, that we may sometimes forget that not all countries have computerized banking operations. The handwritten ledger book still exists. That's why it's critical to know and understand what services you can, and cannot, get in the countries where you want to retire to, or to live in for an extended period.

The Office of International Programs (OIP), a part of the SSA, is responsible for administering the Social Security program outside the United States and for the implementation of the benefit provisions of international agreements. The OIP is assisted by the Department of State's embassies and consulates throughout the world except in the Philippines, where the Department of Veterans Affairs Regional Office (VARO) in Manila assists.

In countries where there are a relatively large number of Social Security customers, American embassies and consulates (and VARO in Manila) have personnel who are specially trained to provide a full range of services, including the taking of applications for benefits. Those countries include:

Argentina	Italy
Australia	Jamaica
Austria	Mexico
Belgium	Netherlands
Costa Rica	New Zealand
Croatia	Norway
Denmark	Philippines
Dominican Republic	Poland
Finland	Portugal
France	Slovenia
Germany	Spain
Greece	Sweden
Hong Kong	Switzerland
Ireland	United Kingdom
Israel	Yemen

Do you reside in Canada, the British Virgin Islands, or Samoa? Obtain services from an SSA field office.

Are you a beneficiary planning to leave the United States to live abroad? Inform the SSA of your change of address before you leave, even if the SSA payments are being sent to a bank. To do so, call 800-772-1213 or contact the SSA field office nearest you, and read *Social Security—The SSA Payments While You Are Outside the United States*, Publication No. 05-10137.

WHEN YOU NEED A SOCIAL SECURITY NUMBER OUTSIDE THE UNITED STATES

Generally, the only individuals outside the United States who are eligible to apply for an original or replacement Social Security card are United States citizens or aliens who have been granted the right to work in the United States by the Immigration and Naturalization Service. If you need a card and are eligible to apply for one, you may obtain an application at any U.S. embassy or consulate. Individuals in the U.S. military may obtain an application from the Post Adjutant or Personnel Office.

A parent who completes an *Application for Consular Report of Birth of a Citizen of the United States of America* completes at the same time an *Application for Social Security Number Card.* Upon approval, the U.S. embassy or consulate sends the application for a Social Security card to the OIP (Office of International Programs) for processing, which takes about forty-five days. It is not necessary for the parent to complete a separate application.

IF YOU'RE NOT ELIGIBLE FOR A SOCIAL SECURITY NUMBER

The Internal Revenue Service (IRS) will issue an Individual Taxpayer Identification Number (ITIN) to nonresident aliens (such as spouses or dependents of U.S. taxpayers) who need a Social Security number for tax purposes, but are not otherwise eligible to have an SSN. An application, Form W-7, may be requested from a U.S. embassy or consulate or by writing to:

> IRS
> Philadelphia Service Center
> ITIN Unit
> P. O. Box 447
> Bensalem, Pennsylvania 19020

WHAT DOES "OUT OF THE UNITED STATES" MEAN?

According to the SSA, you are "out of the United States" when you are not in one of the fifty states, the District of Columbia, Puerto Rico, the U.S. Virgin Islands, Guam, the Northern Mariana Islands, or American Samoa.

After being away from the United States for thirty days in a row, you are considered to be "outside the United States" until you return and stay in the United States or its possessions, as noted above, for at least thirty days in a row.

Not a U.S. citizen? You may have to establish that you were lawfully present in the United States for that thirty-day period. For more information, you may contact the nearest U.S. embassy or consulate or Social Security office.

If you are a citizen of one of the countries listed below, yet eligible for SSA benefits, your payments will be paid no matter how long you stay outside the United States. (*Note*: Countries are subject to change at any time.)

Austria	Japan
Belgium	Korea (South)
Canada	Luxembourg
Finland	Netherlands
France	Norway
Germany	Portugal
Greece	Spain
Ireland	Sweden
Israel	Switzerland
Italy	United Kingdom

> To check on the status of foreign countries and your SSA benefits, call or write:
>
> > Social Security Administration
> > Office of International Programs
> > P.O. Box 17775
> > Baltimore, Maryland
> > 21235-7775
> > 410-966-5416
> > Fax: 410-965-6539
> > or access www.ssa.gov

If you are a citizen of one of the countries listed below (again, subject to change—see box above for a note about getting up-to-date listings), you also may receive your payments as long as you are outside the United States. If you are receiving your payments as a dependent or survivor, that requires additional steps, also listed below.

Albania	Crotia
Antigua and Barbuda	Cyprus
Argentina	Czech Republic
Bahamas	Denmark
Barbados	Dominica
Belize	Dominican Republic
Bolivia	Ecuador
Bosnia-Herzegovina	El Salvador
Brazil	Gabon
Burkina Faso	Grenada
Chile	Guatemala
Colombia	Guyana
Costa Rica	Hungary

Iceland

Macedonia, former
Yugoslav Republic of

Malta

Marshall Islands

Mexico

Micronesia, Federal
States of

Monaco

Nicaragua

Palau

Panama

Peru

Philippines

Poland

Saint Christopher and
Nevis

Saint Lucia

Samoa

San Marino

Serbia-Montenegro

Slovak Republic

Slovenia

Trinidad-Tobago

Turkey

Uruguay

Venezuela

ELIGIBILITY FOR A PENSION FROM A FOREIGN COUNTRY

If you become entitled to a U.S. Social Security retirement or disability benefit and you also start to receive a monthly pension from a foreign country, your U.S. Social Security benefit may be smaller. This applies to pensions provided by foreign countries or private pension based in whole or in part on work not covered by U.S. Social Security. Your local Social Security office can help you figure out the benefits to which you're entitled.

If you are not a citizen of the United States nor a citizen of one of the other countries listed above, your

SSA payments will stop after you have been outside the United States for six full calendar months unless you meet one of the following conditions:

1. You are in the active U.S. military or naval service.
2. The worker on whose record the SSA benefits are based had railroad work that was treated as covered employment by the Social Security program.
3. The worker on whose record the SSA benefits are based died while in the U.S. military service or as a result of a service-connected disability and was not dishonorably discharged.
4. You are a resident of a country with which the United States has a Social Security agreement.

See the box on page 112 for a note about up-to-date listings; currently, countries with Social Security agreements with the United States are:

Austria	Korea (South)
Belgium	Luxembourg
Canada	Netherlands
Finland	Norway
France	Portugal
Germany	Spain
Greece	Sweden
Ireland	Switzerland
Italy	United Kingdom

CLUE: The agreements with Austria, Belgium, Germany, Sweden, and Switzerland permit you to receive benefits as a dependent or survivor of a worker while you reside in the foreign country only if:

1. the worker is a U.S. citizen or a citizen of your country of residence; or
2. you are a citizen of one of the countries listed below and the worker on whose record your benefits are based upon lived in the United States for at least ten years or earned at least 40 earnings credits under the U.S. Social Security system.

Afghanistan
Australia
Bangladesh
Bhutan
Botswana
Burundi
Cameroon
Cape Verde Islands
Central African Republic
Chad
China, People's
    Republic of
Congo Republic
Ethiopia
Fiji
Gambia
Ghana
Haiti
Honduras
India
Indonesia
Kenya
Laos
Lebanon
Lesotho

Liberia
Madagascar
Malawi
Malaysia
Mali
Mauritania
Mauritius
Morocco
Myanmar
Nepal
Nigeria
Pakistan
Saint Vincent and
    Grenadines
Senegal
Sierra Leone
Singapore
Solomon Islands
Somali Democratic
    Republic
South Africa,
    Republic of
Sri Lanka
Sudan
Swaziland

Taiwan	Tonga
Tanzania	Tunisia
Thailand	Uganda
Togo	Yemen

You cannot use this exception if you are not a citizen of one of the countries listed above.

When Payments Stop

Your payments will stop after you have been outside the United States for six months, and they cannot be started again until you return to the United States and stay in the United States for a whole calendar month, if you are not a United States citizen and none of these exceptions applies to you. This ruling is very specific about time: you must be in the United States on the first minute of the first day of a month, and stay through the last minute of the last day of that month. *No exceptions.* If you are not in the country on the first day, the limit is extended to include one full calendar month.

You may also be required to establish lawful presence in the United States for that full calendar-month period. For more information, you may contact the nearest U.S. embassy or consulate or Social Security office.

DEPENDENTS AND SURVIVORS REGULATIONS WHEN LIVING ABROAD

If you are a dependent or a survivor of a worker and you are not a U.S. citizen, you must have lived in the

United States for at least five years, and during those five years, the family relationship on which your benefits are based must have existed. For example, if you are receiving benefits as a spouse, you must have been married to the worker and living in the United States for at least five years.

Children who cannot meet the residency requirement on their own may be considered to meet it if the residency requirement is met by the worker and other parent (if any). Children adopted outside the United States will *not* be paid outside the United States, even if the residency requirement is met.

The residency requirement will not apply to dependents and survivors if:

1. you were initially eligible for monthly benefits before January 1, 1985.
2. you are entitled on the record of a worker who died while in the U.S. military service or as a result of a service-connected disease or injury.
3. you are a citizen of Israel or Japan.
4. you are a citizen or resident of one of the countries with which the United States has a Social Security agreement.

These countries (subject to change, see box on page 112) are:

Austria	Germany
Belgium	Greece
Canada	Ireland
Finland	Italy
France	Korea (South)

Luxembourg	Spain
Netherlands	Sweden
Norway	Switzerland
Portugal	United Kingdom

YOU CANNOT RECEIVE PAYMENTS IN SOME COUNTRIES

The U.S. Treasury Department regulations prohibit sending payments to you if you are in Cambodia, Cuba, or North Korea. You can, however, receive all of your payments that were withheld once you leave any of these three countries and go to one where the SSA *can* send payments. So, in effect, your benefits will always be paid, but will not be sent to where you are if you're in these three countries (or others the Treasury deems too politically unstable). As a safeguard meant for your protection, the benefits will always be held for you for retrieval.

Social Security restrictions prohibit sending payments to individuals in some countries such as Vietnam or areas that were in the former Soviet Union (other than Armenia, Estonia, Latvia, Lithuania, and Russia). SSA payments cannot be sent to anyone for you when you are outside the United States. The SSA will send payments only to a representative payee inside the United States and its posessions.

To obtain more information on how these exceptions affect you and your benefits, write or call:

> Social Security Administration
> Office of International Operations
> P.O. Box 17775

Baltimore, Maryland 21235-7775
410-966-5416
Fax: 410-965-6539

You must be able to speak English. Try to call during normal business hours of Eastern Standard Time (EST) within the United States. (There may be up to a twelve-hour time difference, so always double-check.) There is *no* toll-free 800 number for calls from outside the United States, and the SSA does not accept e-mail transmissions because of privacy issues.

KEEP THE SSA UP TO DATE ABOUT YOUR WHEREABOUTS

Whenever you are living outside the United States and collecting any SSA benefits, the SSA will send you a questionnaire periodically to fill out and return as soon as possible. If you do not do this, your payments will stop.

Again, don't fudge. If you fail to report something or deliberately make a false statement, you could be penalized by a fine or imprisonment. You may also lose some of your payments if you do not report changes promptly.

If you are concerned about reporting in a timely manner, you might consider not having payments sent abroad but, instead, have them sent to a U.S. financial institution (bank, savings and loan, or credit union). Otherwise, your representative payee can handle your affairs while you are gone. Generally speaking, however, if you are close to a U.S. embassy or consulate, your reporting can be done in a timely manner. When you report changes, you can contact the SSA in person, by mail, or by telephone.

If you live in Canada or Mexico, you can send the SSA report to the nearest U.S. Social Security office, U.S. embassy, or consulate.

If you live in the Philippines, the SSA report should be sent to:

> Veterans Affairs Regional Office
> Social Security Division
> 1131 Roxas Boulevard
> 0930 Manila
> Philippines

If you live in other countries, you can report to the nearest U.S. embassy or consulate. To contact the SSA by mail, send the SSA report *by airmail* to:

> Social Security Administration
> P. O. Box 17769
> Baltimore, Maryland 21235-7769
> USA

On *all* of your correspondence to the SSA, you should provide the following information:

1. your name or the name of people you are reporting, such as spouse or other dependents
2. what is being reported and the date it happened
3. Social Security number or claim number on the Social Security check or on correspondence from the SSA

What to Report:

1. change of address
2. disabled person returning to work
3. death
4. incapacity or inability to manage funds
5. marriage
6. divorce or annulment
7. adoption of a child
8. child leaving the care of a wife, husband, widow, or widower
9. changes in parental circumstances
10. eligibility for a pension from work not covered by Social Security
11. child near age 18 is disabled or a full-time student
12. deportation or removal from the United States

When you write to a U.S. embassy or consulate or the Social Security Administration, be specific. List all names and Social Security numbers related to the worker and his or her dependents and/or survivors.

When working abroad, you must report about your job even if it's part time or if you are self-employed. Some examples of the types of work that should be reported are work as an apprentice, farmer, sales representative, tutor, writer, etc. If you own a business, you should notify the SSA even if you do not work in the business or receive any income from it.

If a child beneficiary (regardless of age) begins an apprenticeship, notify the nearest U.S. embassy or consulate or the Social Security Administration. An apprenticeship may be considered work under the Social Security program.

DEPORTATION OR REMOVAL
FROM THE UNITED STATES

If you are deported or removed from the United States, your SSA Social Security benefits may be stopped and cannot be started again unless you are lawfully admitted to the United States for permanent residence. Although you may be deported or removed from the country, and your benefits stopped, this will not affect your dependents, who will continue to receive their entitled benefits, provided that they are U.S. citizens.

If the dependents are not U.S. citizens, they must stay in the United States while you are deported or removed. They can receive benefits only if they are in the United States the entire month for which payments are made. If they spend any part of the month outside the United States, they forfeit their benefits for that month.

THE FOREIGN WORK TEST

A monthly benefit is withheld for each month that a beneficiary, under full retirement age, works more than forty-five hours outside the United States. This applies to work that is employment or self-employment that is not subject to U.S. Social Security taxes. It does not matter how much was earned or how many hours were worked each day.

A person is considered to be working on any day he or she:

1. actually works as an employee or self-employed person.
2. has an agreement to work even if he or she does not actually work because of sickness, vacation, etc.
3. is the owner or part owner of a trade or business even if he or she does not actually work in the trade or business or receive any income from it.

THE ANNUAL RETIREMENT TEST

Under certain conditions, work performed outside the United States by U.S. citizens or residents is covered by the U.S. Social Security program and the same annual retirement test that applies to people in the United States will apply to you.

If you are working for a U.S. company doing business outside the United States, your personnel office will take care of this, whether or not you are also receiving retirement or disability benefits. You are, however, responsible for checking that all taxes are paid on your earnings as described above. It's always a good idea to double-check that your firm's accounting or personnel office is doing the proper paperwork for you. *Never assume.* Doing so may cost you fines and penalties later on.

CLUE: Work by some U.S. citizens and residents outside the United States is *exempt* from U.S. Social Security as a result of international Social Security agreements the United States has with the countries listed below, although the SSA benefits will be subject to the Foreign Work Test.

Austria	Korea (South)
Belgium	Luxembourg
Canada	Netherlands
Finland	Norway
France	Portugal
Germany	Spain
Greece	Sweden
Ireland	Switzerland
Italy	United Kingdom

This list of countries, too, may change at any time. See box on page 112 for a note about up-to-date listings.

And for more information, contact the nearest U.S. embassy or consulate or Social Security office.

If your work is covered by the U.S. Social Security program, you can receive all benefits due you for the year if your earnings do not exceed the annual exempt amount. This limit changes each year, so to find out what the current limit is, ask at any U.S. embassy or consulate or Social Security office.

When your earnings go over the limit, some or all of your benefits will be offset by your earnings.

LOST OR STOLEN SSA CHECKS IN FOREIGN COUNTRIES

Delivery time varies from country to country, and your check may not arrive the same day each month as it ordinarily does in the United States. If you do not receive your check within a reasonable amount of time, or if it is lost or stolen, write for a replacement check immediately.

Contact either the nearest U.S. embassy or consulate or write directly to:

> Social Security Administration
> P.O. Box 17769
> Baltimore, Maryland 21235-7769
> USA

Replacement of lost or stolen SSA checks in foreign countries usually takes considerably longer than it does in the United States, so patience is requested.

SOCIAL SECURITY SERVICES OUTSIDE THE UNITED STATES

The following are embassy, consulate, and other offices around the world that can assist you whenever you need help with matters related to your Social Security benefits or those for your spouse or dependents. As noted elsewhere, whenever you live outside the United States, you must be aware if that country is on the accepted list for SSA benefit payment treaties. Contact your nearest U.S. embassy or consulate if unsure.

Argentina

> Federal Benefits Unit
> U.S. Embassy
> 4300 Colombia
> 1425 Buenos Aires
> Telephone: 541-772-3076
> Fax: 541-777-3437

Australia

Social Security Division
Veterans Affairs Regional Office
U.S. Embassy
1131 Roxas Boulevard
0930 Manila
Philippines
Telephone: 63-2-522-4716
Fax: 63-2-526-4030

Austria

Federal Benefits Unit
U.S. Embassy
Gartenbaupromenade 2, 4th Floor
1010 Vienna
Austria
Telephone: 43-1-31339-7539
Fax: 43-1-513-4351

Belgium

Federal Benefits Unit
U.S. Embassy
27 Boulevard du Regent
B-1000 Brussels
Telephone: 32-2-508-2388
Fax: 32-2-513-0409

Costa Rica

Federal Benefits Unit
U.S. Embassy
Rohmosner 1200
San José
Costa Rica
Telephone: 506-220-3050
Fax: 506-220-2476

Croatia

Federal Benefits Unit
U.S. Embassy
Andrije Hebranga 2
10,000 Zagreb
Croatia
Telephone: 385-1-455-0895
Fax: 385-1-455-0774

Denmark

(Administered by Sweden)
Federal Benefits Unit
U.S. Embassy
Strandvagen 101
S-115 89 Stockholm
Sweden
Telephone: 46-8783-5300
Fax: 46-8667-9109

Dominican Republic

Federal Benefits Unit
César Nicolas Penson
corner to Maximo Gomez
Santo Domingo
Dominican Republic
Telephone: 809-221-5034 or 0232
Fax: 809-562-3559

Finland

(Administered by Sweden)
Federal Benefits Unit
U.S. Embassy
Strandvagen 101
S-115 89 Stockholm
Sweden
Telephone: 46-8783-5300
Fax: 46-8667-9109

France

Federal Benefits Unit
U.S. Embassy
2 Rue St Florentin
75382 Paris Cedex 08
France
Telephone: 33-1-43-12-4705
Fax: 33-1-43-12-4824

or

Federal Benefits Unit
American Consular Agency

31 Rue du Marechal Joffre
06000 Nice
France
Telephone: 33-4-9388-8955
Fax: 33-4-9387-0738

Germany

Federal Benefits Unit
American Consulate General
Siesmayerstr 21
60323 Frankfurt Am Main
Germany
Telephone: 49-69-7535-2496
Fax: 49-69-749-352

Greece

Federal Benefits Unit
U.S. Embassy
91 Vasilis Sophias Avenue
10160 Athens
Greece
Telephone: 30-1-720-2426
Fax: 30-1-646-9885

Hong Kong

Federal Benefits Unit
American Consulate General
26 Garden Road
Hong Kong
Telephone: 852-2841-2483
Fax: 852-2845-4845

Ireland

Federal Benefits Unit
U.S. Embassy
42 Elgin Road
Ballsbridge
Dublin 4
Ireland
Telephone: 353-16-687-122 Ext. 2111
Fax: 353-16-687-245
NOTE: Due to reorganization, Social Security workloads for the Netherlands have been transferred to the U.S. Embassy in Dublin, Ireland. For assistance, please call the U.S. Embassy's Federal Benefits Unit at 353-16-687-122, ext. 2111, or write to the address above.

Israel

Federal Benefits Unit
American Consulate General
27 Nablus Road
Jerusalem 91002
Israel
Telephone: 972-2628-5618
Fax: 972-272-2233

or

Federal Benefits Unit
U.S. Embassy
71 Hayarkon Street
Tel Aviv 63903
Israel
Telephone: 972-3-519-7531
Fax: 972-3-5160744

Italy

Federal Benefits Unit
American Consulate General
Piazza della Repubblica
80122 Naples
Italy
Telephone: 39-81-5838-235
Fax: 39-81-761-1804

or

Federal Benefits Unit
U.S. Embassy
Via Veneto 119/A
00187 Rome
Italy
Telephone: 39-6-4674-2326
Fax: 39-6-4674-2542

Jamaica

Federal Benefits Unit
U.S. Embassy
Jamaica Mutual Life Center
2 Oxford Road, 3rd Floor
Kingston
Jamaica
Telephone: 876-929-4850
Fax: 876-935-6018

Mexico

Federal Benefits Unit
American Consulate General
Chihuahua
Avenue Lopez Mateos 924 Norte
32000 Ciudad Juarez
Mexico
Telephone: 52-16-13-4048
Fax: 52-16-13-46-98

or

Federal Benefits Unit
American Consulate General
Progreso 175
44100 Guadalajara, Jalisco
Mexico
Telephone: 52-3-825-8641
Fax: 52-38-257942

or

Federal Benefits Unit
U.S. Embassy
Paseo de la Reforma 305
06500 Mexico D. F.
Mexico
Telephone: 52-5-209-9100 (ask for Federal
   Benefits)
Fax: 52-5-208-0191

The Netherlands

Because of a reorganization, Social Security cases for beneficiaries living in the Netherlands have been transferred to the U.S. Embassy in Dublin, Ireland. For assistance, please call the U.S. Embassy's Federal Benefits Unit in Ireland at 353-16-687-122, ext. 2111, or write to them at

> Federal Benefits Unit
> U.S. Embassy
> 42 Elgin Road
> Ballsbridge
> Dublin 4
> Ireland

New Zealand

> (Administered by VA/Philippines)
> Social Security Division
> Veterans Affairs Regional Office
> U.S. Embassy
> 1131 Roxas Boulevard
> 0930 Manila
> Philippines
> Telephone: 63-2-522-4716
> Fax: 63-2-526-4030

Norway

Federal Benefits Unit
U.S. Embassy
Drammensveien 18
0244 Oslo
Norway
Telephone: 47-2-2448-550
Fax: 47-2-25527-43

Philippines

Social Security Division
Veterans Affairs Regional Office
U.S. Embassy
1131 Roxas Boulevard
0930 Manila
Philippines
Telephone: 63-2-523-1001
Fax: 63-2-522-1514

Poland

Federal Benefits Unit
American Consulate General
UL. Stolarska 9
31-043 Krakow
Poland
Telephone: 48-12-429-6655, ext. 182
Fax: 48-12-422-4557

or

Federal Benefits Unit
U.S. Embassy AL. Ujazdowskie 29/31
00-540 Warsaw
Poland
Telephone: 48-22-628-3041, ext. 2121 or ext. 2361
Fax: 48-22-625-0289

Portugal

Federal Benefits Unit
U.S. Embassy
Avenida das Forcas Armadas
1600 Lisbon
Portugal
Telephone: 351-21-770-2403
Fax: 351-21-726-8696

Slovenia

(Administered by Croatia)
Federal Benefits Unit
U.S. Embassy
Andrije Hebranga 2
10,000 Zagreb
Croatia
Telephone: 385-1-455-0895
Fax: 385-1-455-0774

Spain

Federal Benefits Unit
U.S. Embassy
Serrano 75
28006 Madrid
Spain
Telephone: 34-91-587-2261
Fax: 34-91-587-2260

Sweden

Federal Benefits Unit
U.S. Embassy
Strandvagen 101
S-115 89 Stockholm
Sweden
Telephone: 46-8783-5300
Fax: 46-8667-9109

Switzerland

Federal Benefits Unit
U.S. Embassy
Jubilaeumstrasse 93
3005 Bern
Switzerland
Telephone: 41-31-357-7235
Fax: 41-31-357-7366

United Kingdom

Federal Benefits Unit
U.S. Embassy
24/31 Grosvenor Square
W1A 2LQ London
England
Telephone: 44-207-499-9000, ext. 2510
Fax: 44-207-495-7200

Yemen

Federal Benefits Unit
Dhar Himyar Zone
U.S. Embassy
Sheraton Hotel District
Sanaa
Republic of Yemen
Telephone: 967-1-238-842
Fax: 967-1-238-870

India Exempt

Social Security benefits paid to individuals who are citizens and residents of India are exempt from this tax to the extent that their benefits are based on federal, state, or local government employment.

DIRECT DEPOSIT WHILE LIVING ABROAD

Direct deposit can also be arranged if you are living abroad. This helps you avoid check-cashing and currency-conversion fees, which can be expensive.

Social Security benefits paid to beneficiaries living abroad are calculated in U.S. dollars. The benefits are not increased or decreased because of changes in international exchange rates.

Foreign countries that accept direct deposit or other electronic payment methods are:

Anguilla	Haiti
Antigua and Barbuda	Hong Kong
Argentina	Ireland
Australia	Italy
Austria	Jamaica
Bahama Islands	Malta
Barbados	Netherlands
Belgium	Netherlands Antilles
British Virgin	New Zealand
Islands	Norway
Canada	St. Lucia
Cayman Islands	St. Vincent and the
Cyprus	Grenadines
Denmark	South Africa
Dominican Republic	Spain
Finland	Sweden
France	Switzerland
Germany	Trinidad and Tobago
Grenada	United Kingdom

HOW TO SIGN UP FOR DIRECT DEPOSIT IN FOREIGN COUNTRIES

To activate a direct deposit account in a foreign financial institution, contact the nearest U.S. embassy or consulate or U.S. Social Security office, or write to:

Social Security Administration
P.O. Box 17769
Baltimore, Maryland 21235-7769
USA

MAJOR CLUE: Many foreign governments *tax* U.S. Social Security benefits, especially those deposited into foreign banks. Any U.S. citizen or alien resident planning to live in another country should contact that country's embassy in Washington, D.C., for information about rights and obligations. If your deposits will be taxed, especially if your benefits are modest, it may be necessary to consider other ways to access your money, or even to consider another place to live.

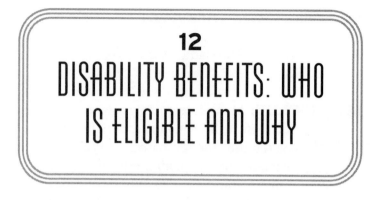

12
DISABILITY BENEFITS: WHO IS ELIGIBLE AND WHY

HOW TO APPLY FOR DISABILITY BENEFITS

Timing is of the essence to receive disability benefits because it does take time (usually six months) to verify your application and determine whether or not you are indeed eligible. Apply as soon as you become disabled, or ask your advocate or representative payee to do this for you.

The Social Security disability waiting period begins with the first full month after the date the SSA decides your disability began. In other words, you apply and wait a few weeks. Then you'll get a decision from the SSA on whether or not you are eligible for disability, and they will choose a date between when you were injured or disabled and when you applied. This could be as few as two weeks or as much as six weeks or longer. You must then wait a month after that before SSI disability benefits are paid, so you can see that timing is of the essence.

The claims process for disability benefits is generally longer than for other types of Social Security benefits, from sixty to ninety days. It takes longer to obtain medical information and to assess the nature of the disability in terms of your ability to work. You can help shorten the process by bringing certain documents with you when you apply and providing other medical evidence you need to show you are disabled. These include:

1. Social Security number
2. birth certificate or other evidence of date of birth
3. military discharge papers, if you were in the military service
4. spouse's birth certificate and Social Security number, if he or she is applying for benefits
5. children's birth certificates and Social Security numbers, if they are applying for benefits
6. checking or savings account information, if benefits are to be directly deposited
7. names, addresses, and phone numbers of doctors, hospitals, clinics, and institutions that treated you and dates of treatment
8. names of all medications you are taking
9. medical records from your doctors, therapists, hospitals, clinics, and caseworkers
10. laboratory and test results
11. a summary of where you worked in the past fifteen years and the kind of work you did
12. a copy of your W-2 Form (Wage and Tax Statement), or if you are self-employed, your federal tax return for the past year
13. dates of prior marriages if your spouse is applying

CLUE: The documents presented as evidence must be either originals or copies certified by the issuing agency. Do not delay filing for benefits just because you do not have all of the information you need. If you do not have a birth certificate, you may request one from the state where you were born.

CLUE: Disability benefits will be paid until you are age 65, if you qualify. After age 65, the disability benefits *automatically* become your retirement benefits without any change to the amount.

If you are applying for Supplemental Security Income (SSI) benefits you also need the following:

1. information about the home in which you live, such as your mortgage or lease and landlord's name
2. payroll slips, bankbooks, insurance policies, car registration, burial fund records, and other information about your income and the things you own

You can apply by calling the SSA toll-free number, 800-772-1213. The SSA representatives there can make an appointment for your application to be taken over the telephone or at any convenient Social Security office. People who are deaf or hard of hearing may call the SSA toll-free TTY number, 800-325-0778, between 7 A.M. and 7 P.M. on Monday through Friday, except holidays.

WHAT IS A DISABILITY?

Social Security defines disability as the *inability to work*. You are disabled if you cannot do the work you did before you were disabled or if you cannot do something else because of your disability/medical condition.

Disability is not a short-term situation but one which is expected to last at least a year or for the life of the applicant, or is expected to result in death. The Social Security Administration is very rigid about this definition. Compensation for short-term disability can be accessed from insurance, workers' compensation, or from the personal savings and investments of the worker or from income from other family members.

The Social Security has written a "Blue Book" to list and define disabilities and medical conditions which warrant long-term disability status. You can review these guidelines online at www.ssa.gov/disability/professionals/bluebook or inquire at your local Social Security office.

HOW THE SSA DETERMINES DISABILITY

The SSA will ask you five basic questions to determine if your disability makes you eligible for benefits. They are:

1. Are you working? If you are and your earnings average more than $700 a month, you generally cannot be considered disabled.
2. Is the condition severe? Impairments must interfere with basic work-related activities for your claim to be considered.

3. Is your condition found in the list of disabling impairments? The SSA maintains a list of impairments for each of the major body systems that are so severe they automatically mean you are disabled. If your disability isn't on the list, the SSA will need to decide if it is acceptable. If it is not, go to the next step.

4. Can you do the work you did previously? If your disability is severe, but not at the same level of severity as an impairment on the list, then you must determine if it interferes with your ability to do the work you did in the last fifteen years. If it does not, your claim will be denied. If it does, your claim will be considered further.

5. Can you do any other type of work? If you cannot do the work you did in the last fifteen years, can you do any other type of work? Your age, education, past work experience, and transferable skills will be reviewed in relation to the job demands of occupations listed by the Department of Labor. If you cannot do any other kind of work, your claim will be approved. If you can still do the work, your claim will be denied.

NAVIGATING *THE DISABILITY REPORT FORM* (SSA-3368)

Of all the services that the Social Security Administration provides, nothing is as complicated as disability. What follows is a synopsis of the information needed to apply for disability.

MAJOR CLUE: For babies born with infirmities, or children who have ongoing mental or physical problems because of lifelong disabilities, the objective is to obtain and sustain disability payments until the child is an adult. Then, the benefits can be disallowed or continued, depending upon the severity and prognosis of the disability.

For adults, most disabilities occur as they age, or from accidents or injuries sustained either on or off the job. The main criterion is whether the disability affects the ability to work at either your previous job or to be retrained for another line of work.

The information requested by the SSA is listed below to give you an idea of the depth and breadth of information you will need to provide. If your claim is denied, you can appeal. (See page 180 for information on the appeals process.)

First and foremost, the SSA will need your name and Social Security number to identify your records. You must list a daytime telephone or the name and telephone number of someone who can reach you quickly. Please make sure that person understands the importance of contacting you immediately whenever they get a call for you about your SSI case.

Friends, relatives, or others aware of your injuries or illnesses may be contacted so that the SSA can have a clearer picture of how your medical condition affects you and your ability or inability to work. In addition, they will ask for reports from doctors and hospitals where you have sought treatment.

Personal information such as height and weight are required because they affect decision making on certain health conditions.

If you have a Medicaid, Medi-Cal, or other medical assistance card issued by your state government, your card number may be needed for your file. (Other health insurance card numbers are not necessary.)

CLUE: If you do not know something asked of you on the form, write DO NOT KNOW. But obviously, the more information you can provide, the quicker your file will be processed.

The SSA can help those who do not speak, read, or write English. You may be provided with an interpreter and/or provided with publications written in your language. (Interpreters for the deaf and hearing impaired are also available.) Helping you understand your rights and obligations is part of the SSA's program.

You will be asked to describe your illnesses, injuries, or conditions; how they affect you; and how they impact your work. Other information needed will be the following:

1. When did the condition begin (exact date if known)?
2. How does it limit your activities?
3. Do you have other illnesses or conditions that affect your work, such as mental or emotional illness, whether or not you are receiving treatment for them?
4. What work, if any, have you performed since the condition first arose?
5. What are the restrictions because of your condition? Do they impact your walking, sitting, lifting, and carrying or ability to carry out instructions (such as memory loss)?

6. What are the symptoms of your condition? (These possibilities include pain, shortness of breath, fatigue, and restrictions for daily activities such as personal care, food preparation, household maintenance, or recreational activities.)

If you have made changes to accommodate your condition at work, please note those changes: working fewer hours, receiving extra help from your employer or coworkers, doing lighter duties, working fewer days, or changing positions within the same company, or stopping working altogether.

Disability Insurance benefits may be retroactive up to twelve months to the beginning of the sixth full month after your disability began. SSI benefits may begin the first month after the date the disability began or the date your application was filed.

Your work record for the last fifteen years will help the SSA determine if you are able to do a job you did previously even if it is not the one you are doing now. You will need to list the job title, type of business, dates you worked, number of hours and days, and your pay rate.

Some of the duties you should list are the machines, tools, or equipment you used; the technical knowledge or skills used; the writing of reports; and any supervising or management of other people you did.

The disability checklist requires a yes or no answer to each of the items. You must also describe your primary job and its main duties. For example, you will also be asked how many hours of each workday you handled large objects; wrote or typed; handled small objects; or walked, stood, sat, climbed, stooped, kneeled, crouched, crawled, or performed other physical duties. How much weight you lifted or carried is important to know to determine if your condition precludes your ability to do that again.

The department will need your medical records for all treatment and medication you received. If you do not have the records, you will be asked to list the medical sources so that the records can be obtained. If you have not received medical treatment, you may be asked to submit to a medical examination.

Your physicians, physical therapists, or psychiatrists are *not* asked to decide if you are disabled; that decision is made by the SSA. However, you must list *all* healthcare professionals you have seen for your illnesses, injuries, or conditions. That can include physicians, psychologists, optometrists, nurse practitioners, physician's assistants, therapists, chiropractors, social workers, and counselors, and alternative medicine professionals, such as acupuncturists.

Give complete addresses and contact numbers; dates of treatment; how long you have been treated; and if and when you have your next appointment. The more specific you are, the faster your claim will be processed.

You must also list names and addresses of hospitals and clinics that have treated you for your illnesses, injuries, or conditions. If a hospital or clinic has more than one location, be specific about which one you used.

Don't remember? Check your appointment card or invoice, or call the doctor or hospital directly.

You will be asked to list the type of hospital or clinic stay, such as:

1. inpatient (if you stayed at least one day overnight)
2. outpatient (if sent home the same day)
3. emergency room treatment (when seen and when sent home)

Do you have a representative payee or an advocate who has your records? They could be state workers' compensation departments, insurance companies, public welfare offices, attorneys, or prisons.

List *all* of the medicines you take, even if they are not for the current illnesses, injuries, or conditions for which you are filing. Note how often you take them, how you are affected, and if they are improving your condition. If you are using over-the-counter medicines, herbs, or homeopathic remedies, list those, too.

Name who prescribed the medicine, why you are taking it (such as to lower blood pressure), and how it affects you (mental or physical side effects).

The department may also request results from MRI/CT scans, X-rays, EEG, EKG, treadmill, cardiac catheterization, biopsy, vision and hearing tests, HIV tests and non-HIV blood tests, breathing tests, and even IQ tests, all of which will determine your ability or inability to perform in your present job.

Your education is important to evaluate, also. List if you have attended classes for specific learning disabilities such as reading or comprehension disorders or classes related to physical disabilities such as deafness or blindness. They will be considered in the evaluation.

Vocational training is also an element in the decision to allow disability payments. If you have attended sheltered workshops, met with job coaches, or received job training, coaching, or evaluation services related to your work life, please list them, including all the details of names, addresses, contact numbers, and personnel.

For more information, go to www.ssa.gov; read *Disability,* Publication No. 05-10029; or access www.ssa.gov/pubs/10029. It is available in Spanish—*En Español:* Publication No. 05-10929 and at www.ssa.gov/Espanol/10929.html.

Should you disagree with the decision by the SSA about your disability, an appeals process is available. (See page 180 for information on how to appeal.)

CLUE: Some conditions occur over time; others are sudden such as a heart attack. The SSI reviews all scenarios.

CLUE: You may be eligible for SSI benefits even if you have never worked.

CLUE: Do not falsify anything on this application. Not only will it affect whether you receive benefits, but you may also be subjected to fines or imprisonment.

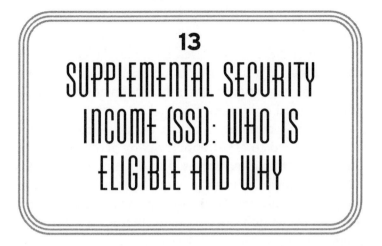

13

SUPPLEMENTAL SECURITY INCOME (SSI): WHO IS ELIGIBLE AND WHY

Supplemental Security Income (SSI) is a Social Security program that provides stipends to people with limited income and resources. The assistance is very modest (the average is $512 per month) and is not meant to be the sole source of anyone's income; rather, it is meant as a *supplement* in times of hardship, or for those people unable to work, temporarily or permanently.

Not only is SSI a modest benefit, but it is also subject to discounting if you are a wage earner, self-employed, or have other sources of income. There is also a catch-22 element: To qualify for this assistance, you can't own much, earn much, or do much to bring in more income.

Still, for those on the edge or completely in the depths of poverty, SSI is a help financially. SSI also opens up access to other benefits programs such as food stamps (except in California), plus Medicaid medical assistance for doctors' bills, prescription drugs, hospital visits, and other healthcare costs.

The eligibility requirements are pretty straight-forward because the program is aimed at helping the indigent and disenfranchised on all levels. One can be homeless or in a shelter without a permanent address, be an asylee or a new immigrant, or someone suddenly incapacitated or without funds.

The SSI counselors at the Social Security office are all trained to assist applicants by acquiring documentation, filling out forms, and opening up the lines of communication until they are back on their feet or until their condition or illness improves. For those with permanent conditions, such as blindness, SSI payments can continue until death.

WHAT ARE THE ELIGIBILITY REQUIREMENTS?

To be eligible for SSI benefits as an adult, you must be age 65 or older, blind, or disabled. Children eligible for SSI benefits must be blind or disabled, and either a minor younger than 18 or a student between 18 and 22 years old, and must not be married.

Disabled Adults

1. 65 or older; or
2. blind (20/200 vision or less in your better eye with best correction; or your visual field is 20 degrees or less, even with a corrective lens); or
3. disabled; and
4. with limited income; and
5. a U.S. citizen or one of certain qualified aliens; or a resident of the United States, including the

District of Columbia, and the Northern Mariana Islands (see below for details); and

6. agrees to apply for other benefits; and meets certain other requirements
7. unable to work due to a physical or mental impairment which has lasted or is expected to last at least twelve months or result in death

Disabled Children

1. younger than 18 with a physical or mental condition or conditions that can be medically proven and that have resulted in marked and severe functional limitations; or
2. age 18 to 22 and a student; or
3. age 18 to 22 with the adult disability definition or condition(s) that have lasted or will last at least twelve months or end in death

CITIZENSHIP QUALIFICATIONS

Citizenship plays a unique factor in qualifying for SSI benefits. The recipient must be a U.S. citizen; however, an alien can qualify if the "qualified alien" category is met as per 1996 legislation, and if the qualified alien meets all the other eligibility requirements for income and resource limits and/or health limits.

Who is a "Qualified Alien"?

A qualified alien is a person who is or has been:

1. Lawfully Admitted for Permanent Residence (LAPR) in the United States, which includes

"Amerasian immigrants," as defined in Section 584 of the Foreign Operations, Export Financing and Related Programs Appropriations Act of 1988.

2. granted conditional entry under Section 203(a)(7) of the Immigration and Nationality Act (INA) as in effect prior to April 1, 1980.
3. paroled into the United States under Section 212 (d)(5) of the INA for a period of at least one year.
4. a refugee admitted to the United States under Section 207 of the INA.
5. granted asylum under Section 208 of the INA and given asylee status.
6. a person whose deportation was withheld under Section 241(b)(3) of the INA.
7. a Cuban/Haitian entrant under Section 501(e) of the Refugee Education Assistance Act of 1980.
8. subjected to battery or extreme cruelty, or has a child or parent who has been subjected to battery or extreme cruelty (certain circumstances apply).

You Must Meet One of the Following "Exceptions"

Your SSI eligibility may be limited to seven years, or extended longer, provided you meet one of these exceptions or/and you are in one of the alien categories.

1. You have been receiving SSI since August 22, 1996, and lawfully residing in the United States.

2. You are an LAPR with 40 qualifying quarters of work.
3. Your spouse or parent has performed work that counts toward 40 quarters of work for receiving SSI only. (Note: Quarters of work earned *after* December 31, 1996, cannot be counted if you, your spouse, or your parent received certain benefits from the U.S. government based on limited income and resources during that period.)
4. You entered the United States for the first time on or after August 22, 1996. You might not be eligible for SSI for the first five years as an LAPR, even if you have 40 qualifying quarters of earnings. (Consult with the SSA to verify your eligibility.)
5. You are an active-duty member of the U.S. Armed Forces or an honorably discharged veteran, or
6. You are the spouse or widow(er) or dependent child of an active-duty member of the U.S. Armed Forces or an honorably discharged veteran.
7. You are blind or disabled and have lived legally in the United States.
8. You became a refugee under Section 207 of the INA.
9. You sought asylum under Section 208 of the INA.
10. You became an alien whose deportation was withheld under Section 243(h) of the INA or whose removal is withheld under Section 241(b)(3) of the INA.

11. You are/were a Cuban/Haitian entrant under Section 501(e) of the Refugee Education Assistance Act of 1980.

Native American Exception

Some categories of noncitizens may be eligible for SSI yet not subject to the August 22, 1996, Law for Certain Non-Citizens. They are:

1. American Indians born in Canada who are under Section 289 of the INA; or
2. American Indians who are members of a federally recognized Indian tribe under Section 4(e) of the Indian Self-Determination and Education Assistance Act.

WHERE AN SSI BENEFICIARY LIVES MATTERS

To be eligible to receive SSI benefits you must:

1. live in any of the fifty U.S. states, the District of Columbia, or the Northern Mariana Islands; or
2. be a child living with a parent in the military service assigned overseas to permanent duty ashore; or
3. be a student temporarily abroad for the purpose of conducting studies.

WHAT ARE THE SSI DEFINITIONS OF INCOME AND LIMITED INCOME?

Income is defined for SSI as money you earn from a job or business or other sources such as Social Security; Department of Veterans' Affairs; friends or relatives; and free food, clothing, or shelter from friends, relatives, or community agencies.

While income is what you earn, resources are defined as what you own, such as land, personal property, life insurance, and/or cash/bank accounts.

The limits are $2,000 for individuals and $3,000 for couples. If a child under 18 lives with one parent, $2,000 of the parent's total countable resources do not count. If the child lives with two parents, $3,000 do not count. Other categories of resources include:

1. anything else you own which could be changed to cash and used for food, clothing, or shelter
2. some of the resources of a spouse, parent, or sponsor of an alien

What Are the Other Requirements?

To be eligible for SSI benefits, you must also apply for all benefits or payments that you are also eligible for including pensions, Social Security, and/or vocational rehabilitation services if you are blind or disabled and under age 65.

WHO IS INELIGIBLE FOR SSI BENEFITS?

Fugitive felons who are fleeing criminal charges, trials, avoiding custody, or who are in violation of probation or parole may not be eligible for SSI benefits.

Anyone who is in jail cannot receive SSI benefits even if they were eligible before incarceration.

Selling your personal property or other resources for *less* than they are worth so that your case appears eligible for benefits is not acceptable and could delay benefits for up to three years. Giving away your personal property to imply that you do not own these items is also discouraged by the SSI.

HOW MUCH ARE SSI PAYMENTS?

For the year 2001, the federal SSI benefit rate was $530 per month for an individual and $796 per month for a couple, and benefits increase slightly each year.

States have many options when it comes to administering supplemental funds to SSI beneficiaries. Among these options are the right to provide any benefits at all, to give or not give food stamps, to administer the program, to share the administrative tasks with the Social Security Administration, or to give it wholly to the SSA to handle. Those states that contribute benefits to the federal supplement may choose the amount, which can be as little as $15 a month—and based not only on your circumstances but on the wealth of the state in which you live.

The following do *not* pay benefits:

Arkansas	Northern Mariana Islands
Georgia	Tennessee
Kansas	Texas
Mississippi	West Virginia

The SSA administers the state supplement in the following states:

California	Nevada
Delaware	New Jersey
District of Columbia	New York★
Hawaii	Pennsylvania
Iowa★	Rhode Island
Massachusetts	Utah
Michigan★	Vermont★
Montana	Washington

★Dual administration state. Both the SSA and these states administer a state supplement.

The following states pay and administer supplemental payments:

Alabama	Missouri
Alaska	Nebraska
Arizona	New Hampshire
Colorado	New Mexico
Connecticut	North Carolina
Florida	North Dakota
Idaho	Ohio
Illinois	Oklahoma
Indiana	Oregon
Kentucky	South Carolina
Louisiana	South Dakota
Maine	Virginia
Maryland	Wisconsin
Minnesota	Wyoming

WHAT RESOURCES ARE "ALLOWED"?

The following assets are *not* counted by the SSI in the $2,000–$3,000 limit categories:

1. the home you live in and the land it is on
2. household goods and personal property that are not worth more than $2,000
3. one wedding ring and one engagement ring
4. burial spaces for you or your immediate family
5. burial funds for you and your spouse, each valued at $1,500 or less
6. life insurance policies with a combined face value of $1,500 or less
7. one car, regardless of value, if it is:
   a. necessary for employment or medical treatment
   b. modified for use or transportation of a disabled person
   c. necessary because of climate, terrain, distance, or similar factors to perform essential daily activities. Otherwise, up to $4,500 of the market value of your car is *excluded.* The remaining value of the car *is* counted against the resource limit of $2,000 for an individual and $3,000 for a married couple.
8. property essential to self-support, such as resources that a blind or disabled person needs
9. support and maintenance assistance and home energy assistance
10. cash received for medical or social services for one month, except cash reimbursement of

expenses already paid out by the beneficiary
and considered regular income
11. state or local relocation assistance payments
for nine months
12. crime victim's assistance for nine months
13. earned income tax credit payment for the
month following receipt
14. dedicated accounts for disabled or blind
children
15. disaster relief assistance
16. cash received for the purpose of replacing an
excluded resource that is lost, damaged, or
stolen (such as a home)
17. property in a trust that meets the
requirements for a Medicaid payback trust or
a Medicaid pooled trust
18. retroactive SSI or Social Security payments
for up to six months after you receive them
(including payments received in installments)

INSTALLMENTS DEFINED

When eligible for certain large past-due SSI payments,
after Interim Assistance Reimbursement has been
paid, individuals will receive these payments in installments rather than in one lump sum payment, but in no
more than three payments at six-month intervals. The
amount of the first and second payment may be increased because of certain debts.

There are two lump-sum exceptions:

1. if you have a medical condition that is
expected to result in your death within twelve
months

2. if you become ineligible for SSI and are likely to remain ineligible for twelve months

CAN I SELL A RESOURCE?

You may be able to get SSI while you are trying to sell your resources, but when they sell, you must pay back the SSI payments, referred to as "conditional payments." You must also sign a "conditional benefits agreement," which is subject to acceptance by the SSA before a conditional payment period can begin.

HOW DOES THE SSI DEFINE "INCOME"?

The SSI has four definitions of income: earned, unearned, in-kind, and deemed.

1. Earned income is money from the wages from a job or the earnings from self-employment.
2. Unearned income is money from SSA, pensions, state disability, unemployment benefits, interest income, and cash from friends and relatives or similar sources.
3. In-kind income is food, clothing, or shelter that is either free or less than the fair value.
4. Deemed income is money from people you live with or who support you in some way such as income of your spouse, parent with whom you live, or sponsor (of an alien). This income is used by the SSA to compute the amount of your SSI payment.

WHAT INCOME IS NOT COUNTED BY THE SSI?

1. the first $20 of most income received in a month
2. the first $65 of earnings and one-half of earnings over $65 received in a month
3. the value of food stamps
4. income tax refunds
5. home energy assistance
6. assistance based on need funded by a state or local government
7. small amounts of income received irregularly or infrequently
8. food, clothing, or shelter based on need provided by nonprofit agencies
9. loans to you (cash or in-kind) that you have to repay
10. money someone else spends to pay your expenses for items other than food, clothing, or shelter, for examples, if someone pays your telephone or medical bills
11. income set aside under a Plan for Achieving Self-Support (PASS)

HOW DOES THE SSA FIGURE OUT THE SSI BENEFIT AMOUNT?

To determine your SSI benefit amount, the SSA first determines your countable income by subtracting any income not counted from your total income, usually the first $20 you earn. Then the countable income is subtracted from the current SSI federal benefits rate. What remains is your monthly benefit amount.

For example: Marvin earns monthly SSA benefits of $300, his total income. When applying for SSI, the first $20 of his income is not counted, leaving Marvin a "countable" income of $280. He is eligible for the SSI benefit rate of $530, so his countable income will be adjusted this way: $530 in SSI benefits, less his SSA countable income of $280, which gives him a net SSI benefit of $250. His total monthly income is no longer $300, but is now $530—an increase of $230. As you can surmise, SSI benefits are a *supplement* to current income, with qualifiers.

Total monthly income = $300 (SSA payment)

1.	$300	(SSA payment)
	-20	(credit, not counted)
	$280	(countable income)
2.	$530	(SSI federal benefit rate)
	-280	(countable income)
	$250	(net SSI payment)

New total monthly income = $530 ($280 + $250)

Marvin's brother Bob is still working and earns $400 per month. Because he is working, he gets two deductions, a $65 credit as a wager earner *and* the $20 not counted amount. That changes his countable income from $400 (-20) to $380 (-$65) to $315. Then, the SSA subtracts an additional 50 percent as non-counted income, so his actual countable income becomes $157.50 ($315 x 50% = $157.50).

The first $65 of earnings and one-half of earnings over $65 received in a month are deducted from SSI recipients who are wage earners.

Total monthly income = $400 (wages)

$400
<u>-20</u>   (not counted)
$380
<u>-65</u>   (wage earner credit; not counted)
$315 x 50 percent = (additional wage earner credit)
= $157.50 countable income

$530.00   (SSI federal benefit rate)
<u>-157.50</u>   (countable income)
$372.50   (net SSI payment)

New monthly income is now $677.50

These "credits" are awarded because he is gainfully employed and attempting to earn an income. Because the income is so low, Bob qualifies for the SSI benefit of $530, from which his net income of $157.50 is subtracted to make his net SSI benefits $372.50 ($530 - $157.50 = $372.50). That makes his total income $315.00 plus $372.50 or $677.50; certainly a boost.

HOW DOES THE DEEMED INCOME CATEGORY APPLY?

Deemed income is that income received by someone who lives with you such as a spouse, parent, child, or sponsor if you are an alien. The SSA may count some of the sponsor's income against that of the benefit for the alien. It may also count some of a spouse's income in figuring your SSI payment (if the spouse is *not* eligible for SSI). Some of the parents' income may also be counted toward the account of a disabled child under 18 who lives with his or her parents (if the parents are not eligible for SSI).

Deemed income no longer applies when:

1. a beneficiary no longer lives with a spouse or parent.
2. a disabled or blind child reaches age 18.
3. the sponsor of an alien dies.

HOW DO "LIVING ARRANGEMENTS" AFFECT SSI BENEFITS?

Your living arrangement—where you live and how, with whom you live and how they do or do not contribute to the household—determines how much SSI benefits you can receive.

Some of the possibilities of the SSI's definition of "living arrangements" are:

1. in your own house, apartment, or trailer
2. in someone else's household
3. in a communal situation such as a board and care facility or institution

The following living arrangements may mean reduced SSI benefits for you:

1. You live in another person's house, apartment, or trailer, and you pay only a part of your share of your food or housing costs.
2. You live in a house, apartment, or trailer, and someone else pays for all or part of your food,

rent or mortgage, utilities, and other services such as garbage removal.

3. You are in a hospital or nursing home for the whole month and Medicaid pays for over one-half of the bill.

4. You are in an institution run by a federal, state, or local government for the whole month.

MAJOR CLUE: You cannot get any SSI benefits if you are in some form of government institution unless Medicaid is paying more than half of your bills. However, if you will be in a medical institution for ninety days or less, you may receive SSI benefits.

WHAT IF YOU VIOLATE PROBATION OR PAROLE?

You are not eligible to receive SSI in any month in which you violate federal or state parole or probation.

WHAT IF YOU'RE HOMELESS?

You do not need an address to be eligible for SSI. You receive benefits "as if" you lived in your own house or apartment or trailer. If you live in a public shelter designated for the homeless, you may receive the maximum allowance your state provides for up to six months during any nine-month period, subject to renewal.

SSI FOR CHILDREN

The SSI does not have a minimum age for SSI eligibility. Anyone disabled or blind may receive benefits, even if married or head of a household.

The SSI does, however, apply maximum age limits. A child is defined as one who is neither married nor head of the household and is under age 18; or under age 22 and a student regularly attending school or college or training that is designed to prepare the person for a paying job.

If the child has a physical or mental condition or conditions that can be medically proven and which result in marked and severe functional limitations such as blindness; or the condition(s) have lasted or are expected to last at least twelve months or end in death, benefits will continue until that time (twelve months or death). If 18 to 22 years old, the SSI will apply the adult disability definition.

Does Deemable Income Apply to a Child?

Yes. If a child is under age 18, not married, and lives at home with parents who do *not* receive SSI payments, the parents' income or resources may be made available to the child, or what the SSI calls "deeming."

Deeming and Public Income Maintenance

SSA does not consider the income of a parent for deeming purposes if the parent receives a public income maintenance payment such as Temporary Assistance to Needy Families (TANF).

After deductions for the income of parents and for other children living in the home are subtracted, the amount remaining is used to decide if the child meets the SSI income requirements for a monthly payment. If either the child or the parent is not living in the household temporarily, the deemed income still applies. Deeming will stop when the child becomes 18 years old, or is no longer living with the parent on a permanent basis.

Other exceptions to deeming are when:

1. a disabled child who received SSI while in an institution goes to live at home.
2. the child is eligible for Medicaid under a state home care plan.
3. deeming would otherwise cause ineligibility for SSI.

If the above applies, SSA may pay up to $30 per month plus state supplements, as applicable.

Medical Benefits and SSI Child Beneficiaries

A child who gets SSI can get Medicaid to help pay medical bills in most, but not all, states. A child may also be eligible for Medicaid while in an institution but not eligible when living at home because parental resources are too high; however, in some states, minors who live at home may keep Medicaid eligibility while getting home care if that care is less costly to the government. States vary considerably on this issue, so please refer to the SSI rulings in your state, plus any other services they may provide.

Children of Armed Forces Personnel Living Overseas

Children living with a parent in the military overseas may receive SSI but are not eligible for Medicaid, which is based on an individual physically living in the United States with the intention of remaining there permanently or for an indefinite period.

Dedicated Accounts and Children

When an eligible child under age 18, who has a representative payee, is eligible for certain large past-due payments covering more than six months of benefits, these payments must be paid directly into a separate account in a financial institution. This separate account is referred to by the SSA as a "dedicated account" because funds in this account are dedicated (may only be used) for certain expenses, primarily those related to the child's disability and maintained separately from any other banking account set up for the children.

DEEMING ELIGIBILITY INFORMATION

The Social Security Administration (not the state) supervises the state supplement for children in the following states. Please consult them about eligibility and other regulations.

California	Massachusetts
Hawaii	Michigan
Iowa	Montana*

Nevada★★	Rhode Island
New Jersey	Utah
New York	Vermont
Pennsylvania	Washington

★Montana supplements disabled and blind children in certified foster homes only.

★★Nevada supplements blind children only.

MAJOR CLUE: All states have the right to administer supplemental income as they see fit.

State-Administrated Supplement

If you live in one of the states listed below, your state (not the Social Security Administration) supervises the state supplement for children.

Alabama	Nebraska
Arizona	New Hampshire★
Colorado	New Mexico
Connecticut★	North Carolina
Idaho	North Dakota
Illinois	Oklahoma
Kentucky	Oregon★
Louisiana	South Dakota★★
Maine	Wisconsin
Minnesota★	Wyoming

★Connecticut, Minnesota, New Hampshire, and Oregon supplement payments only to blind children.

★★South Dakota supplements disabled and blind children in residential care facilities.

NOTE: All other states do not administer supplements to children.

HOW TO APPLY FOR SSI BENEFITS

You can call, write, or visit any Social Security office to begin the process of eligibility for SSI benefits, or a representative payee or social worker can assist you. Be prepared to provide substantial information and the SSA will assist you in completing all the forms. When completed, you must sign an application.

As with all benefit applications, timing is important. The sooner you apply, the sooner you will receive benefits. When you call to make an appointment with the SSA, that date will be considered your application filing date. Failure to keep your appointment may mean reapplication.

If you are leaving a public institution in a few months, you may not be eligible for SSI until you actually leave, but you may be able to apply for the benefits while you are still in the institution. The SSA calls this a "prerelease procedure," and your institution and the SSA can help you make the filing.

 MAJOR CLUE: All these application services are free and the SSA is available to help you apply, complete forms, and get the documents you need to meet all eligibility requirements. If you do not have all the information, begin the process anyway, because the sooner you apply, the sooner you will get the benefits.

WHAT ABOUT DISABLED AND BLIND APPLICANTS?

The SSA decides what medical information is needed to make a decision; it will pay for you to see a doctor and may pay transportation costs to take any medical exam. You may appoint someone to go with you to your appointment(s) with the SSA or the medical examiner. The representative can:

1. help you complete forms.
2. go with you to the local SSA office.
3. interpret for you. (The SSA may alternatively provide an interpreter for you. Minors are not permitted to interpret for you. "Interpreter" also means interpreters for the deaf or hard of hearing. All these services are free.)
4. help gather forms or information.
5. accompany you to medical examinations or to the SSA office.
6. receive mail for you at his or her address.

A representative payee can also:

1. review your file at the SSA office.
2. get information from SSA about your claim, just as you can.
3. represent you at informal or formal hearings.
4. give SSA evidence for you.
5. help you with appeals.

For more information on what a representative payee can do, see chapter 6 or request the *Appointment of Representative Form,* SSA-1696.

 MAJOR CLUE: A representative's duties are different from those of a representative payee. Ask the SSA for information on the Representative Payment Program, which explains the differences.

DOCUMENTS YOU MAY NEED WHEN YOU APPLY FOR SSI

The SSA will tell you what documents are necessary to file your claim, and the list varies for different types of situations. Some, but not all, of the documents you may need include:

- Social Security card
- proof of age (birth certificate, public or religious birth record before age 5 or similar document showing your age). If you already proved your age when you applied for Social Security benefits, you do not need to prove it again for SSI benefits.
- citizenship or alien status (birth certificate showing you were born in the United States, religious record of birth or baptism showing your place of birth in the United States, naturalization certificate, U.S. passport, or certificate of citizenship)

If you are an alien, the following are examples of documents you may need:

- current (unexpired) Immigration and Naturalization document; e.g., an I-551 (Permanent Resident Card); or
- I-94 (Arrival/Departure Record)
- If you have served in the U.S. Armed Forces, you may need your military discharge paper (Form DD-214).
- proof of income (either earned income in the

form of payroll stubs, or if self-employed, a tax
return, or unearned income in the form of any
records you have (such as award letters, bank
statements, court orders, or receipts, showing
how much you receive, how often, and the
source of the payment)
- proof of resources (such as bank statement(s)
  for all checking and savings accounts, deed or
  tax appraisal statement for all property you own
  besides the house you live in, insurance policies,
  and certificates of deposit, stocks, or bonds)
- proof of living arrangements (such as a deed or
  property tax bill, lease or rent receipt, medical
  assistance cards for all household members, or
  information about household costs, food,
  utilities, etc.)
- medical sources (including medical reports, if
  you have them, and names, addresses, and
  telephone numbers of doctors and other
  providers of medical services, if you are applying
  as a blind or disabled person)

For Caregivers

If you are applying for benefits for a disabled child, the
SSA needs the names, addresses, and telephone numbers of people (teachers, caregivers) who can provide
information about how the child's condition affects his
or her day-to-day activities. If you are applying for
benefits for a disabled or blind adult, the criteria listed
below must be completed.

MAJOR CLUE: Documents must be originals; photocopies are not acceptable. All will be returned to you.

Disabled or Blind Applicants

You will be asked to explain your disability. The SSA will ask for the following information:

1. what your disability is, how it affects your ability to work, how it affects your ability to function in your daily activities, and how long it has bothered you
2. medical treatments you have had or any medicines you take
3. names, addresses, and phone numbers of doctors and other providers of medical services
4. dates of treatment, and clinic or patient identification numbers
5. names and addresses of hospitals and dates of inpatient and outpatient treatment
6. names and addresses of persons who know how your condition affects your day-to-day functioning
7. schools you have attended
8. dates, places, and types of work you have done in the past fifteen years

WORKERS WHO REQUIRE SSI

Each SSA office has a Work Incentive Liaison who works with outside organizations that serve disabled and blind people. Please contact your local office for the name and telephone number of the Work Incentive Liaison and ask them about impairment-related work expenses, rules for blind people who work, and individual development accounts. You can also read more details about the benefits in the following publications: *Plans for Achieving Self Support; Property You Need for Self Support; Student Child Earned Income Exclusion;* and *Continued Medicaid Eligibility for People Who Work,* Section 1619(b).

The Red Book on Work Incentives (also available on audiocassette) contains additional information on both SSI and Social Security disability work incentives. Call 800-772-1213 for copies of any of these books or publications.

REPORTING CHANGES THAT AFFECT YOUR SSI BENEFITS

You must report all the changes listed below to your SSA office within ten days after the end of the month in which the event occurs. Timing is critical because the changes may affect your eligibility. Failure to do so or reporting falsely may mean loss of benefits, the requirement to repay benefits received, or a fine.

1. change of address
2. change in living arrangements
3. change in income
4. change in resources
5. death of a spouse or anyone in your household
6. change in marital status
7. eligibility for other benefits and/or payments

8. admission to or discharge from an institution (hospital, nursing home, prison, or jail)
9. change in school attendance
10. leaving the United States

Information to Report If You Are Disabled

1. medical improvement
2. refusal to accept vocational rehabilitation services if referred
3. a return to work

Whenever the SSA sends you a notice, it is because it contains something you should know about your benefits, claims, or payments and what, if any, action to take. *Do not ignore it.* Blind beneficiaries will also receive notices by mail unless they request a complementary phone call or notices by certified mail. The SSA will provide Braille notices, upon request.

Notices are currently available in Spanish, upon request, and notices in other languages will be made available in the future as demand indicates. If you misplace an SSA notice, call and request another. If you do not understand it, call for an explanation. Whatever you do, never ignore a notice from the SSA.

REDETERMINATIONS

The word "redetermination" is SSA-speak for reviewing a case to determine the beneficiary's continuing eligibility. Some recipients are selected within three months after benefits are awarded but most are redetermined once every one to six years. Reporting a change, such as marriage, may affect eligibility or payment, your income, resources, and living arrangements and may subject your case to review (or redetermination by mail, phone, or in person).

If you do not respond in a timely fashion, usually thirty days, your checks may stop, you may be under- or overpaid (subject to repayment by you of any overpayment), or you may lose your Medicaid eligibility.

What Causes an Overpayment?

An overpayment is the difference between what you were paid and what you were due for any month. Some of the more common reasons for an overpayment are:

- Your income is more than you estimated.
- Your living situation changes.
- You have more resources than the allowable limit.
- You are no longer disabled and continue to receive payments.
- You do not report a change to SSA (on time or at all) as required.

If the SSA incorrectly figures your payments because of incorrect/incomplete information, it will send you a notice explaining the overpayment and ask for a full refund within thirty days. If you are currently getting checks and do not make a full refund, the SSA will withhold 10 percent of your total income until the repayment is made.

Should you believe you were not overpaid, you may request a reconsideration. When you ask for an appeal within ten days of the date on the notice, the SSA will not reduce your payment until they make a decision.

If you do agree that an overpayment was indeed made but not because of anything you did, you may ask for a waiver of overpayment. When granted a waiver by the SSA, you will not have to repay the over-payment.

If your overpayment is verified, but you do not have the funds to repay the amount, you can ask the SSA to waive it by demonstrating that you need the money to meet ordinary living expenses, or demonstrate that your bills will use up your income and cause a hardship.

CLUE: You have a right to review your file. It may help you demonstrate that the overpayment wasn't your fault. Keep *all* records, correspondence, and copies of your SSI benefits check in a special file to check against your file in the SSA office.

APPEALS PROCESS

You can appeal any SSA decision considered an initial determination. The issues are whether or not you are eligible, how much the SSI payment amount should be, and whether you must repay an overpayment.

You or your representative may contact the SSA to file an appeal and pursue the appeals process. For more information, see *How Someone Can Help You with Your SSI.*

Reconsideration

If you disagree with the initial determination, you may request reconsideration by writing within sixty days of when you receive the initial determination to SSA or by completing Form SSA-561 (*Request for Reconsideration*) or Form SSA-789 (*Disability Cessation Appeal*).

If you ask for reconsideration within ten days, any payment the SSA is currently making will continue until the SSA makes a decision. If you appeal a disability cessation, you must request benefit continuation for the SSA to send you a notice of the reconsideration decision.

You are entitled to a face-to-face hearing with a disability hearing officer if your disability has abated.

Hearing

If you disagree with the reconsideration decision, you or your representative may request a hearing before an administrative law judge by writing to the SSA or by completing Form HA-501 (*Request for Hearing*). The SSA will help you complete this form.

A hearing must be requested within sixty days after you get the notice of reconsideration, and you may review your file before the hearing and/or add new evidence to the file at this time.

You may ask the judge to make a decision based on the evidence in your file, but you (or your representative) must appear in person at any scheduled hearing. If for any reason you cannot make it, contact the judge immediately and explain why. If you do not attend the scheduled hearing, you may lose your appeal rights and benefits.

If you have to travel more than seventy-five miles one way, the SSA may pay you for travel costs, but you must tell the judge *before* the hearing that you need travel expenses paid for by the SSA.

To hear cases of disability, the judge may ask for more medical exams or tests, or you may request additional medical exams or tests if you think you need more medical information. The judge decides whether to grant your requests, and may ask other witnesses, such as doctors, to come to the hearing. You may ask the judge to request specified witnesses to attend the hearing on your behalf.

During the hearing, the judge will explain your case and may ask you and any witnesses questions. You or your representative have the right to ask any witnesses questions and present new evidence.

Although the hearing is informal, it is recorded and you have the right to ask for a copy of the recorded hearing. Upon making the decision, the judge will send you (and your representative) a copy of the hearing decision.

Appeals Council

If you disagree with the judge's decision, you or your representative may request an appeal in writing within sixty days after you receive the decision. Contact the SSA and request an Appeals Council review or complete Form HA-520 (*Request for Review of Hearing Decision/Order*). The SSA will help you complete this form.

The Appeals Council will examine your case and will grant, deny, or dismiss your request for review. If the Appeals Council grants your request for review, it will either decide your case or return it to the judge for further action: another hearing and a new decision. The Appeals Council will send you and your representative a copy of its decision and an explanation of it.

CLUE: You or your representative may enter any new evidence into your file for the Appeals Council to consider.

Federal Court

If you disagree with the action of the Appeals Council, you may file a civil action with the U.S. District Court in your area, but you must seek legal aid or a lawyer to assist you as the SSA cannot help you file a court action. You must file an action in federal court within sixty days after you receive the Appeals Council decision. The Federal Court will review the evidence and the previous decisions and make a final judgment. It does not, however, conduct a hearing.

WHAT IF YOU NEED PAYMENTS FOR AN EMERGENCY?

The SSA can make an emergency advance check payment to new applicants who face a financial emergency, before any regular payment is authorized. Only one such advance payment can be made. The emergency advance cannot be higher than the SSI federal benefit rate (plus any federally administered state supplement). If SSA is not able to make a presumptive disability decision, sometimes the DDS will make one if it has sufficient information for a final decision.

EXPEDITED PAYMENTS

There are three different situations in which payments are made more quickly than usual:

1. presumptive disability or blindness payment
2. emergency advance payment
3. immediate payment

Presumptive disability or blindness payments are available for up to six months if you applied for SSI because of a disability or blindness and are waiting for the DDS to make a final decision. The SSA can make a presumptive disability or blindness decision if you have one or more of the following medical conditions:

1. amputation of two limbs
2. amputation of a leg at the hip
3. allegation of total deafness
4. allegation of total blindness
5. allegation of bed confinement or immobility without a wheelchair, walker, or crutches, allegedly due to a long-term, continuing condition, excluding recent accident and recent surgery
6. allegation of cerebral palsy, muscular dystrophy, or muscular atrophy and marked difficulty in walking (use of braces), speaking, or coordination of the hands or arms

7. allegation of diabetes with amputation of a foot
8. allegation of Down syndrome
9. an applicant filing on behalf of another individual alleges severe mental deficiency for claimant who is at least seven years of age
10. HIV (human immunodeficiency virus) infection
11. allegation of a stroke (cerebral vascular accident) more than three months in the past with continued, marked difficulty in using arms or legs
12. infants who weighed less than 1,200 grams at birth, or less than 2,000 grams at birth and they were "small for gestational age."

WHO CAN RECEIVE AN EMERGENCY ADVANCE PAYMENT?

1. people who will receive presumptive disability or blindness payments
2. people who are likely to meet all SSI eligibility requirements
3. people facing a "financial emergency" who need money right away due to a threat to health or safety, such as not enough money for food, clothing, shelter, or medical care

When your SSI is approved, SSA will *deduct* the emergency advance payment from the payments already due you and pay you the difference. The SSA will subtract your payment in up to six monthly installments if you are not due past payments.

If your benefits are denied and the emergency advance payment was for presumptive disability or blindness, you will not be asked to repay; in all other cases, you will.

The SSA can make an immediate payment directly to an individual if there is eligibility and payment is already due. SSA office management makes this decision based on its own sense of discretion.

Applicants and those already receiving SSI who are fully eligible and who face a financial emergency and have no other option are the only people who can receive emergency payments from SSI/SSA.

SSI AND ELIGIBILITY FOR OTHER GOVERNMENT PROGRAMS

Medicaid

In most states, if you are an SSI recipient, you may be automatically eligible for Medicaid and you may not need another application. In other states, you must apply for and establish your eligibility.

Food Stamps

The Food Stamp Program provides help for low-income households to buy the food needed for good nutrition and overall health. If you are applying for or already receive SSI, you can get Food Stamp information and an application form at your local SSA office. (It is possible for all the members of your family to get their own SSI and Food Stamp allocation. Ask the SSA office for recertification or more information.)

CLUE: SSI payments count in computing Food Stamp eligibility. Some states, like California, do not offer Food Stamps for SSI recipients.

Temporary Assistance to Needy Families (TANF)

The TANF program provides cash block grants to states along with the ability to determine TANF eligibility rules and to set TANF payment amounts. Your Social Security office can make a referral for you to participate in this program.

Health Insurance for Children

Medicaid provides free health coverage to most low-income children; however, many states have added a Children's Health Insurance Program that provides more coverage, especially aimed at health care for minors. Contact your local Medicaid agency, social service office, or welfare office for more information. (The SSA does not administrate this program.)

Local or State Assistance

Some states offer state or local assistance based on need to aged, blind, and disabled people through the State Welfare Department. You may be required to apply for SSI; if granted SSI benefits, the local benefits assistance may stop. And your state may be entitled to collect on any retroactive SSI payments to offset money they paid you while your SSI claim was being processed.

CLUE: States pay the Medicare premiums for people who receive SSI if they are also eligible for Medicaid.

Medicare

You may qualify for assistance with some Medicare costs if:

1. you already receive Medicare.
2. your income is limited.
3. your resources are less than $4,000 for an individual or $6,000 for a married couple.

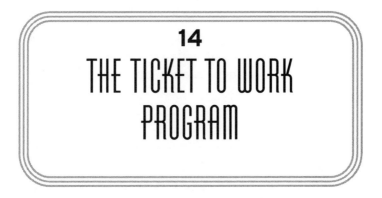

14
THE TICKET TO WORK PROGRAM

TICKET TO WORK AND WORK INCENTIVES IMPROVEMENT ACT OF 1999

On December 17, 1999, President Bill Clinton signed into law the Ticket to Work and Work Incentives Improvement Act of 1999 (Public Law 106-170). The basic purposes of this new law are to:

1. provide health care and employment preparation and placement services to individuals with disabilities to reduce their dependence on cash benefit programs.
2. encourage states to adopt the option of allowing individuals with disabilities to purchase Medicaid coverage that is necessary for these individuals to maintain employment.
3. provide individuals with disabilities the option of maintaining Medicare coverage while working.
4. establish a Ticket to Work and Self-Sufficiency Program that allows Social Security disability and disabled or blind SSI recipients to seek the

employment services, vocational rehabilitation services, and other support services needed to obtain, regain, or maintain employment and reduce their dependence on cash benefit programs.

Substantial Gainful Activity (SGA) is the final objective of the program; that point when disabled individuals are working at optimal level in relation to their disability. The objectives of this program are straightforward and a sincere effort to supplement the dignity and self-esteem of those with disabilities who can work. Like many benefits programs, it can affect existing benefits, reducing them in proportion to outside earnings or pensions. Still, it is hard to dismiss the value of vocational training, job placement services, and the genuine opportunity to participate in the workplace, however modestly.

Recognizing that disabled workers may not be able to do a thirty-five- to forty-hour workweek for forty-eight to fifty weeks a year, the program requires that beneficiaries need only work three months out of twelve in the third year and six months out of twelve in succeeding years.

The time to prepare for employment is generous, too: beneficiaries have a total of two years and nine months, usually sufficient preparatory time even if they are incapacitated for some portion of it.

Beneficiaries also have the option of placing their "ticket" in inactive status during the initial two-year period following assignment if they expect to be unable to participate in their employment plan for a significant period of time.

Any period the ticket is inactive will not count toward the time limitations. Also, the beneficiary will not be subject to a continuing disability review. The program as it stands now requires that, in the third and fourth years, both SSA disability beneficiaries and SSI disabled and blind beneficiaries are required to work at the Substantial Gainful Activity (SGA) level applicable to nonblind beneficiaries for the specified number of months. This level is currently $700 a month.

SSI disability and blindness beneficiaries, Social Security disability beneficiaries who are in a trial work period, and Social Security disability beneficiaries who are statutorily blind, meet the requirement to work at the SGA level applicable to nonblind beneficiaries if their gross earnings from employment, before any exclusions, are at or above the dollar amount of the nonblind (SGA) level, or if their net earnings from self-employment, before any exclusions, are at the SGA level applicable to nonblind beneficiaries ($700).

Earnings at the SGA level applicable to nonblind beneficiaries may not be sufficient to eliminate the payment of all disability benefits, because the amount of earnings needed depends on a variety of factors. Those include whether the beneficiary receives Social Security or SSI benefits, or both, whether the beneficiary is blind or has impairment-related work expenses or is eligible for other income exclusions. Earnings requirements for the third and fourth years are at the SGA level for nonblind beneficiaries to establish an initial earnings level that:

1. is consistent across different categories of beneficiaries, increasing simplicity.

2. allows beneficiaries time to work toward the higher levels of earnings that may be required to eliminate the payment of disability benefits for the required months.

In the fifth and subsequent years, both Social Security and SSI beneficiaries would be required to work for at least six months with earnings in each such month that were sufficient to eliminate payment of Social Security disability and federal SSI cash benefits in a month. All services are free; access to employment, vocational rehabilitation, or other support services will be paid for by the SSA when the beneficiaries achieve certain levels of work.

CLUE: The Substantial Gainful Activity (SGA) levels and benefits are subject to change; please contact your local SSA office each year if they have not sent you any communication about requirements or changes. The program is so new that the "fifth year" will not occur until 2004, and adjustments to the program may be made at any time.

For more information about these proposed rules, contact:

> Geoffrey Funk, Team Leader, Legislative Implementation Team
> Office of Employment Support Programs
> Social Security Administration
> 6401 Security Boulevard
> Baltimore, Maryland 21235-6401
> 410-965-9010 or TTY 800-988-5906

For information on eligibility or filing for benefits, call the SSA national toll-free number, 800-772-1213, or TTY, 800-325-0778, or access www.ssa.gov.

CLUE: Participating states will add their spin to the program. The beneficiary does not have to complete the nine-month continuous period of Substantial Gainful Activity (SGA) prior to January 1, 2004, in order for the costs of the services to be payable under the programs for payments for VR services. The nine-month SGA period can be completed after January 1, 2004. SSA will not pay an alternate participant under these programs for the costs of any services provided after December 31, 2003.

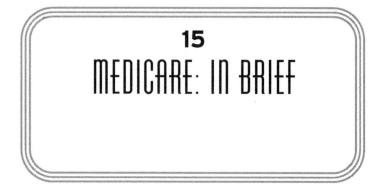

15
MEDICARE: IN BRIEF

WHAT YOU NEED TO KNOW ABOUT MEDICARE

Medicare is a health insurance program for eligible people who are age 65 or over, or are disabled or have kidney failure. Medicare protection consists of two parts: hospital insurance and medical insurance.

The hospital insurance part of Medicare pays hospital bills and certain follow-up care after you leave the hospital. Medical insurance helps pay doctor bills and other medical services. The hospital insurance part of Medicare (sometimes called Part A) pays in-patient hospital bills and certain follow-up care after you leave the hospital. If you are already receiving Social Security benefits when you turn 65, your Medicare coverage will begin automatically.

If you are not already receiving Social Security benefits, you must apply for Medicare by calling the Health Care Financing Administration at 800-MEDICAR(E). Ask for the handbook, *Medicare and You.* Or view this at www.medicare.gov. You can also read *The Medicare Handbook*, HCFA Publication No. 10050, or access www.ssa.gov/pubs/10050. For Spanish, see *En Español,* HCFA Publication No. 10950, or access www.ssa.gov/espanol/10950.

MEDICAL INSURANCE

Medical insurance (sometimes called Part B) is an optional service that helps pay doctor bills and other medical services. Medical insurance requires a premium that you must pay for yourself. Medicare generally does not cover health services you get outside the United States. The hospital insurance part of Medicare is available to you if you return to the United States. No monthly premium is withheld from the SSA benefit payment for this protection.

If you want the medical insurance part of Medicare, you must enroll and there is a monthly premium that normally will be withheld from your payment. Since Medicare benefits are available only in the United States, it may not be to your advantage to sign up and pay the premium for medical insurance if you will be out of the United States for an extended period. But you should be aware that your premium, when you do sign up, will be 10 percent higher for each 12-month period you could have been enrolled but were not.

To obtain the medical insurance part of Medicare, you must enroll and there is a monthly premium that normally will be withheld from your payment. To cancel medical insurance, you should notify the SSA immediately. Medical insurance—and premiums—will continue for one more month after the month you notify the SSA that you wish to cancel it.

People who are deaf or hard of hearing may call

the toll-free TTY number, 800-325-0778, between 7 A.M. and 7 P.M. on business days.

All of these publications are available at any local Social Security office or access them at www.ssa.gov.

To cancel the insurance, you should notify the SSA immediately. Medical insurance—and premiums—will continue for one more month after the month you notify the SSA that you wish to cancel it.

Medicare is a *huge* subject; in fact, it's enough to fill a book! For a detailed analysis of Medicare, how to apply for it, how to get the most out of it, and how to supplement it, please read *Medicare for the Clueless: The Complete Guide to Government Health Benefits,* by Joan Harkins Conklin, also available from Citadel Press.

CLUE: Read More About It:

 Medicare, Publication No. 05-10043
www.ssa.gov/pubs/10043.html
En Español: Publication No. 05-10943
www.ssa.gov/Espanol/10943.html

HOW TO FIND A LOCAL OFFICE

Social Security Administration
Office of Public Inquiries
6401 Security Boulevard
Room 4-C-5 Annex
Baltimore, MD 21235-6401

If you get Medicare and have a low income and few resources, your state may pay your Medicare premiums plus, in some cases, it will pay other Medicare expenses such as deductibles and co-insurance. Only your state can decide if you qualify. To find out if you do, contact your local welfare office or Medicaid agency.

For more information about the program, contact Social Security and ask for a copy of the publication *Medicare Savings for Qualified Beneficiaries*, HCFA Publication No. 02184, or access it at www.ssa.gov/pubs.02184.html.

HCFA (HEALTH CARE FINANCE ADMINISTRATION) PROGRAMS

HCFA provides a number of programs which you may qualify for; to find out what these are, contact your Medicaid agency, social service office, or welfare office. The SSA does not make any of these decisions. They are totally state-run.

1. Qualified Medicare Beneficiary (QMB). This program helps low-income Medicare beneficiaries by paying Medicare premiums, deductibles, and co-insurance.
2. Specified Low-Income Medicare Beneficiary (SLMB) or Qualifying Individuals (QI1 and QI2) programs pay Medicare Part B premiums only and the QI2 program pays only part of the Medicare Part B premium.
3. Qualified Disabled Working Individual (QDWI) program pays Medicare Part A premiums. If you are under age 65, disabled, and no longer entitled to free Medicare Hospital Insurance Part A because you have returned to work, you

may be eligible for a program that helps pay your Medicare Part A monthly premium. To be eligible, you must:

1. continue to have a disabling impairment.
2. sign up for Premium Hospital Insurance (Part A).
3. have limited income.
4. have resources worth less than $4,000 for an individual and $6,000 for a married couple and not already be eligible for Medicaid.

CLUE: Resources do not include the home where you live, one car, and certain insurance.

SOCIAL SECURITY ENTITLEMENT REQUIREMENTS

Many people who are eligible for SSI may also be entitled to receive SSA benefits. Workers must be:

1. age 62 or older, or disabled.
2. "insured" by having enough work credits. Work is measured in "Social Security credits" and you can earn up to 4 credits per year based on your annual earnings. For SSA disability benefits, you need 20 credits in the ten years prior to the start of your disability. Those disabled before age 31 usually need fewer credits to qualify.

BENEFICIARIES

You can earn benefits if you are either age 62 or older or disabled, and your spouse can earn benefits if she or he is:

1. age 62 or older.
2. divorced and age 62 and older, and you were married at least ten years prior to your divorce.
3. under age 62 and caring for a disabled or blind child under age 16 who is receiving benefits on your work record.

A surviving spouse is:

1. a widow(er) age 60 or older.
2. a widow(er) age 50 or older and disabled.
3. divorced and age 60 or older (age 50, if disabled), and was married to you for at least ten years prior to your divorce.
4. under age 60 caring for a child under age 16 or disabled, who is receiving benefits on your earnings record.

Other beneficiaries are:

1. unmarried children (including stepchildren, adopted children, and in some cases, grand-children and illegitimate children) who are: under age 18 (or between ages 18 and 19 if a full-time high-school student); or older than 18 and who became disabled before age 22.

2. dependent parent(s), age 62 or older, of deceased workers.

MAJOR CLUE: To avoid delays in reaching an SSA representative, do not call during their busiest times, which are the day after a holiday, Mondays and Tuesdays, early in a month, and high-traffic hours of 10 A.M. to 3 P.M. Calling off-hours and off-days will get you quicker results. For urgent matters, however, *call immediately.*

16
OTHER SSA-RELATED SERVICES

THE SOCIAL SECURITY ADMINISTRATION SPEAKS YOUR LANGUAGE!

The Social Security Administration provides a number of its publications in both English and Spanish, and a few in other languages to assist new immigrants to the United States. If you know of someone who needs an interpreter, the SSA will provide one free for any of the following languages: Arabic, Armenian, Chinese, Farsi, French, Greek, Haitian-Creole, Italian, Korean, Polish, Portuguese, Russian, Spanish, Tagalog, and Vietnamese. Not all languages are spoken at all SSA offices, but every effort will be made either in person or by phone to engage an interpreter for anyone needing one to handle their Social Security needs. For more information, access www.ssa.gov/multilanguage/ LangPost.pdf.

Hispanics and Social Security

Because Spanish is the most popular second language of Americans and alien residents, the Social Security

Administration has gone to great lengths to ensure that they can read about services for Social Security, Disability, Supplemental Social Income, and other programs in Spanish. For a complete list of publications printed in Spanish, see page 275.

SSA has also devoted an entire page aimed at Hispanic women on its Web site in addition to the publications in Spanish online. For general information written in Spanish for services for men, women, and children, access: http://ssa-spanish.custhelp.com/cgi-bin/ssa_Spanish.

For the page for Hispanic women, access: http://www.ssa.gov/espanol/mujeres/.

NEW SSA NUMBERS FOR NEW IDENTITIES

To answer the needs of the millions who have encountered domestic violence, violence on the streets, hate crimes, and other attacks on their lives, the SSA will, in many cases, offer a new Social Security number to help these people protect their lives with another identity.

One of the first steps is to develop a path to safety. This can include gathering personal papers and putting them in a safe place and choosing a safe house to turn to such as a shelter, a home unknown to the assailant, or to any number of service agencies who deal with domestic violence and victims of violent crimes. If the incidents have been reported to the police, they can be of some assistance, but the best defense is leaving a violent situation as soon as you can.

Social Security does not assign new numbers to replace old ones routinely, but they will do what they can when shown that enough evidence indicates that you are in an abusive situation that endangers your life or the lives of children. Assigning you a new Social Security number is not protection from abuse, of course, but it is a tool to help change identity. Engaging the courts and other legal and social agencies, such as the Department of Justice, is critical to complete the process.

To apply for a new Social Security number, you must go to the Social Security office in person with a statement explaining why you need one, and a completed application for an SSN. Please bring the following with you:

1. original documents of age, identity, and U.S. citizenship or lawful alien status, such as a birth certificate and a driver's license
2. one or more documents identifying you by both your old and new names if you have changed your name (as the Department of Justice recommends)
3. a demonstration of evidence, such as court custody papers, showing that you have custody of your children
4. original documents indicating your children's Social Security numbers, and applications for new numbers for each of them
5. evidence, such as police reports, court papers, or medical treatment reports demonstrating that you may have been abused or harassed. If you need more evidence, your local Social Security office will help you.

WHAT IS EVIDENCE OF VIOLENCE, AND WHO CAN HELP?

Members of the police, doctors and other medical practitioners, and other interested third parties can help you by describing to the SSA the nature and extent of harassment, abuse, or endangerment to your life or those of your family.

Correspondence that is acceptable includes court-approved restraining orders and letters from shelters, family members, friends, counselors, or witnesses who have knowledge of the domestic violence or abuse or the endangerment to your life and those of your family.

CONFIDENTIALITY IS KEY

All Social Security numbers and records are kept confidential by the SSA and never provided to third parties.

How does anyone get your number? Whenever you give it out, and because that happens so often, be careful about sharing your number with those who ask for it, even when it's appropriate. Discretion and caution are particularly critical if you should obtain a new Social Security number to leave an abusive situation.

For more information, call your local Social Security office or call toll-free at 800-772-1213. People who are deaf or hard of hearing may call the toll-free TTY number, 800-325-0778 between 7 A.M. and 7 P.M. on business days.

CLUE: Need help with a violent or abusive situation NOW? Call National Domestic Violence Hotline at 1-800-799-SAFE (7233) or 1-800-

787-3224 (TTY). They will direct you to a safe house or to an agency that can protect you today.

WHAT PRISONERS AND THEIR FAMILIES SHOULD KNOW ABOUT SOCIAL SECURITY

Being incarcerated impacts not only your own life, but those of your family and loved ones. One of the impacts is the possible loss of benefits. Both Social Security and Supplemental Security Income (SSI) benefits are not payable to you during the months that you are incarcerated because you have either been charged or found guilty of a crime. Release from jail does not mean your benefits will be resumed either.

Who Can Get Benefits?

If you are a recent parolee or are unemployed, you are *not* qualified to collect disability or Social Security and no benefits will be payable to you while you are incarcerated.

CLUE: Social Security disability benefits can be paid only to people who have recently worked and paid Social Security taxes, and who are unable to work because of a serious medical condition that is expected to last at least a year or result in death.

NOTE: Social Security retirement benefits can be paid only to people who are 62 or older. Generally, you must have worked and paid taxes into Social Security for ten years to be eligible. When released from prison, some people may be eligible for retirement benefits. Check with your local Social Security office to see if you can qualify.

You cannot collect SSI benefits for any month you are incarcerated. NOTE: SSI benefits can be paid to people who are 65 or older or blind or disabled and who have low income and few resources. If you have been released from prison and fit the requirements for SSI benefits, you may apply for them at your local Social Security office.

To Get Benefits, You Must Apply for Them

You cannot receive benefits while you are incarcerated, or in certain public institutions. However, your spouse and/or children may collect benefits if they are eligible. If you think your spouse or children are eligible, have them apply for benefits at the local Social Security office. For more information, read *What Prisoners Should Know About Social Security*, Publication No. 10133, or access www.ssa.gov/pubs/ 10133.html; *En Español*, Publication No. 10933, or access www.swww. ssa.gov/espanol/10933.

THE APPEALS PROCESS

The following information applies to the appeals process for disability claims that are acceptable only in the following locations: Alabama; Alaska; Colorado; Louisiana; Michigan; Missouri; New Hampshire; Pennsylvania; North and West Los Angeles, California; and Albany and Brooklyn, New York.

Sometimes, despite the investigation of the Social

Security Administration and the urgency of your claim, your benefits to Social Security and/or Supplemental Security Income (SSI) will be denied. The denial to your request is made via a letter to you which explains the decision of the agency. At that time, if you do not agree with the decision, you can ask for an appeal, which in effect is a "second look" at your case. Your local Social Security office can help you arrange for the appeal, and, happily, decisions are sometimes reversed.

WHAT YOU NEED TO KNOW TO BEGIN THE APPEALS PROCESS

Make your appeals request, in writing, within sixty days from the date that you receive the letter in which your benefit request was denied. In most cases, it is assumed that the date of receipt is five days after the letter is dated.

Appeals have three steps or levels of approach:

1. hearing by an administrative law judge
2. review by the Appeals Council
3. federal court review

You can arrange your Social Security appeals with assistance from your local office. *This service is free.* You can also choose an attorney, friend, or other representative to arrange the appeals process for you. Your representative *cannot* charge or collect a fee from you without first getting written approval from Social Security.

Hearing on Denial of Disability Benefits

If you disagree with the initial decision, you may ask for a hearing on the issues of your disability claim, such as whether or not you are disabled, when your disability began, or whether or not it has ended. An administrative law judge who had no part in the first decision of your case will conduct the hearing.

The hearing is usually held within seventy-five miles of your home and you will be notified of the time and place of the hearing by the administrative law judge. You and your representative, if you have one, may attend the hearing and explain your case. You may read through the information in your file, add new information to it, and request that inaccurate information be changed.

You will be asked questions by the administrative judge (who may also question any witnesses).

You may ask questions of the witnesses, or have your representative do so.

Attending the hearing in person demonstrates an active interest in your case, but you do not have to attend. You do, however, have to write a letter explaining why you cannot attend.

After the hearing, the administrative law judge will make his or her decision and the Social Security office will send you a copy of this decision. That decision may also be appealed, using the Appeals Council.

Appeals Council

The Appeals Council reviews all requests for review, but it does not have to have a hearing if it believes that the original decision is correct. If it does review your case, it can either return it to an administrative law judge for more review, decide your case on its own, or let it stand as is. The Social Security office can arrange this step in the appeals process and it will give you a copy of the council's decision on your case or its request to send it back to an administrative law judge for additional review.

If you still disagree, or the council decides not to review your case, you can take your case to Federal District Court by filing a lawsuit.

For more information, read *The Appeals Process,* Publication No. 05-10141. For more information about a representative for your case, read the factsheet, *Social Security and Your Right to Representation,* Publication No. 05-10075. Both are available from any local office, or by calling toll-free 800-772-1213.

ADDITIONAL BENEFITS MAY BE AVAILABLE TO SOME FILIPINO WORLD WAR II VETERANS

Public Law 106-169 was enacted on December 14, 1999, to provide benefits for Filipino veterans who served in the military of the Philippines while those forces were in active service with the U.S. Armed Forces from September 16, 1940, through July 24, 1947, or who served in the organized military of the Philippines from July 26, 1941, through December 30, 1946.

To be eligible, veterans must have been 65 or older on December 14, 1999. Other qualifications include:

1. being a Filipino World War II veteran as described above

2. filing an application for the special Filipino veterans' benefits
3. being eligible for Supplemental Security Income (SSI) for December 1999
4. being eligible for SSI for the month you apply for the special benefits, and having other benefit income that is less than 75 percent of the current SSI federal benefit rate

When Do These Special Benefits Start?

A Filipino veteran who meets all the requirements will be entitled to these special benefits for each month in which he or she is residing *outside* the United States starting on the first day of the month. Qualified veterans will receive a monthly benefit equal to 75 percent of the current SSI federal benefit rate less the amount of the veteran's benefit income for the month.

No provision for payment was made for dependents or survivors.

"Benefit income" means annuities, pensions, retirement, or disability benefits the veteran received during the twelve-month period immediately before applying for special benefits or those paid later but earned during that previous twelve-month period. The current SSI federal benefit rate is $530 per month, effective January 2001.

CLUE: The Filipino veteran's total other monthly benefit income must be less than $397.50 per month or 75 percent of $530 benefit amount.

To apply, bring the following paperwork to your local Social Security office:

1. birth certificate
2. proof of citizenship or alien status
3. tax returns or proof of your other income
4. military discharge papers or Form 14 for military service in World War II
5. military discharge papers or similar proof of service in the organized forces of the Commonwealth of the Philippines
6. proof of foreign residence once you leave the United States

For more information, please read *Special Benefits for Certain World War II Veterans,* Publication No. 05-10157, or access www.ssa.gov/pubs/10157. Interpreters in Tagalog are available, and the publication is available in Tagalog, both by request. If you are now living in the Philippines, contact the SSA Division of the Veterans Affairs Regional Office in Manila:

SSA Department of Veterans Affairs
1131 Roxas Boulevard
0930 Manila
The Philippines

If you are residing elsewhere outside the United States, contact the nearest U. S. embassy or consulate. If you are still living in the United States, contact any Social Security office.

CLUE: For more information about SSI, see chapter 13.

YOUR SOCIAL SECURITY STATEMENT

The SSA has been sending a Social Security Statement on a regular basis only since October 1999. It is sent to every American age 25 and older about three months prior to your birthday. It shows information about earnings on which you have paid Social Security tax (FICA), your insured status for Social Security benefits, and an estimate of your benefit amount at various ages.

So that your online request can remain confidential, SSA uses a security protocol called Secure Sockets Layer (SSL) for this application. You must use a Web browser that supports SSL. Netscape Navigator and Microsoft Internet Explorer are two browsers that support SSL. Using this security protocol, all information sent between your computer and the server is encrypted before being sent on the Internet.

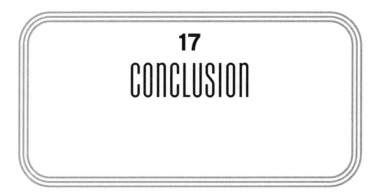

17
CONCLUSION

This Nation must not break faith with those Americans who have a right to expect that Social Security payments will protect them and their families . . .

—President Richard Nixon, September 25, 1969

As demonstrated in *Social Security for the Clueless,* benefits are paid to millions of Americans based on earnings, disability, or dependency. The outlay, according to statistics in 2001, was as follows:

- more than $400 billion in benefits to more than 45 million Americans
- more than $24 billion (an average of $844 per month per person) for the 28.5 million people in retirement. Nearly $1.5 billion was paid in benefits for more than 3 million dependents
- more than $8 billion were paid to either disabled workers or their dependents. About 5 million disabled workers received an average of $786 per month for a total of $4 billion, and their 1.6 million dependents received $4 billion.

Note: Because it is estimated that three out of every 10 Americans will be disabled at least once, this figure will skyrocket as the population continues to grow.

- more than $5 billion in other survivors benefits, averaging $810 per month per person, were given to 7 million other beneficiaries, most of whom are widows and dependent or disabled children.

Despite the impressive list of benefits shown above, it is easy to believe poverty is still very much with us, and particularly too much a part of the lives of the elderly. As the following quote indicates, some things do not change:

> *In this so-called "twentieth century of civilization," in this, the richest country in the world, we find men and women past the age of 65 compelled to surrender their self-respect and become dependent as charitable wards, either on the community or on relatives or friends who in many instances are as badly off as those who depend upon them. Old age dependency is definitely and positively one of the great tragedies of modern economic progress . . . the only way they can subsist and save themselves from penury, hunger, and want, is for them to join the great caravan that finally wends its way over the hill to the poorhouse.*

> —From the House speech made by
> Congressman William Sirovich (D-NY)
> on April 16, 1934, on behalf of the
> Social Security Act of 1935

There is much good news, however. Poverty levels among the elderly have eased since 1935: not as drastically as Social Security claims, yet not as horribly as some news media would have us believe. Ferreting out the truth about poverty is difficult since many people living below the poverty line are rarely "accounted for" in agency research for the government because they are homeless, in shelters, in institutions that may or may not give accurate records, and may be living with friends or family members who do not count them as permanent dependents.

What is poverty? In wealthier communities, poverty may be an income of $4,000 a month; in poorer communities, poverty may be an income of $500 a month, or less. The average monthly retirement benefit is now $700. Is there really anywhere in the United States today that an individual can cover the bulk of their monthly expenses for under $700?

The SSA reports that the poverty rate for elderly Americans has dropped from 35 percent (in 1959) to less than 10 percent (in 1999), yet 18 percent, or about one in five elderly Americans, depend on their Social Security benefits for their *sole* source of support. It does not take a mathematician to realize that 18 percent is nearly twice that of the 10 percent poverty rate among the elderly estimated by the SSA, and this figure does indeed challenge whether or not anyone could live soley on benefits from Social Security and not be considered at or below the poverty level.

Two-thirds of aged Social Security beneficiaries receive 50 percent or more of their income from Social Security, which averages about $700 per month. That translates to 84 percent of those receiving Social Security retirement benefits depending on this money for half to all of their income (66 percent or two-thirds plus 18 percent).

Granted, benefits will increase with time, and the longer you work and the more you earn, the more your Social Security benefits will be, but the lesson to be learned here is that Social Security retirement benefits should *always* be considered a *part* of your retirement portfolio; not the majority and certainly not its entirety.

While it remains true that Social Security is a relatively new program in the history of our country, it is and will always be an *insurance* program for which you contribute a premium in the form of taxes (FICA). Some of us will not live to enjoy the benefits, but the "insurance" will, instead, benefit our minor or disabled children and/or our spouse as they rebuild their lives after their loss. Social Security benefits are, and always will be, an adjunct to savings, stocks, bonds, real estate, or other investments. It should not be considered the ultimate insurance or financial protection for our old age. It behooves all of us under retirement age to plan *today* for retirement.

By 2030, there will be twice as many older Americans as today—from 35 million in 2001 to 70 million in 2030. The trust fund that holds our benefit monies has more than $30 *trillion* now and that, too, will continue to grow. The concern is not that our benefit money will not be there for us but, rather that the amount of benefits will not be all that we will need.

The SSA has developed disability, supplemental income, and other programs to meet our other needs; Medicare is still in place, but as always, the responsibility for our lives and our financial health rests with us. That means we must vigorously invest, save, and conserve our income as conscientiously and as consistently as possible throughout our working lives.

The information and direction provided in *Social Security for the Clueless* have been designed to answer the most common questions about retirement benefits and other services of the Social Security Administration. If you need more answers, or if you and your loved ones need support because of a disability or serious financial concerns, help is but a phone call away: 800-772-1213.

Appendix I
VITAL STATISTICS INFORMATION

Many states have records for birth and death registrations that date back to the 1700s or 1800s; however, several states achieved statehood only during the twentieth century. The older records may be a delight to historians, but have no relevance to Social Security. What does have relevance is the gradual conversion from ledger records to computerized records as a tracking system to ferreting out your original birth certificate or registration of divorce or death. What may be of some concern is that some record keeping dates only since the 1950s, particularly for some U.S. possessions. The clerk will be able to direct you to other sources for your records.

The Hall of Records or Vital Statistics offices listed below offer birth and death certificates, but most do not keep certificates for marriage and divorce papers. Those are frequently kept in the Hall of Records or Clerk's Office of the county in which the marriage was performed and/or the divorce was decreed. Because there are thousands of counties, they are not listed here, but the clerk of any Hall of Records can usually direct you to the corresponding agency in the county where you need to get your records.

Fees are correct as of 2001, but are subject to change at any time. If it's possible, ask for two certified copies "just in case." Some agencies even give a discounted price for multiple copies.

PRELIMINARY QUESTIONS TO ASK

1. Does the agency make certified copies of birth and death certificates?
2. Are records kept for _____ (the years needed for your copies)?
3. What is the current fee?
4. Does the agency accept a personal check? If a check is not acceptable, what form of payment is acceptable? Certified check? Money order? Other?
5. To whom should you make out the check? (This varies considerably from the department name to the state treasurer to the state itself. Ask!)
6. Is a self-addressed stamped envelope needed?
7. What form of identification from you is needed to expedite the request?
8. Is it possible to obtain more than one certified copy?
9. Is there anything else I must do to obtain this certified copy?
10. Does the agency keep records for marriages and divorces? If not, what is the telephone number and address for those agencies?

CLUE: Use the same checklist above for inquiries to obtain certified divorce decrees and marriage certificates.

ADDRESSES AND TELEPHONE NUMBERS FOR U.S. VITAL STATISTICS BUREAUS

Most telephone numbers below give recorded messages. Please have pad and pencil in hand to jot down the information. If you have a question not answered by the recording, please note any referral numbers given to you, or write to the address given.

CLUE: Some states have their own Web sites for vital statistics and they are listed below. The SSA also maintains a list online. For the most up-to-date information about your state's fees, access http://www.cdc.gov/ nchs/data/w2w11_99.pdf. To write or call, contact

National Center for Health Statistics
Division of Data Services
6525 Belcrest Road
Hyattsville, MD 20782-2003
301-458-4636

Alabama

Center for Health Statistics
State Department of Public Health
P.O. Box 5625
Montgomery, AL 36103-5625
334-206-5418
www.alapubhealth.org
Fees range from $12 and up.

Alaska

Department of Health and Social Services
Bureau of Vital Statistics
P.O. Box 110675
Juneau, AK 99811-0675
907-465-3391
Fees are $10 and up.

American Samoa

Registrar of Vital Statistics
Vital Statistics Section
Government of American Samoa
Pago Pago, AS 96799
684-633-1222, ext. 214
For divorce papers write to
High Court of American Samoa
Tutuila, AS 96799
Fees are $1 and up.

Arizona

Vital Records Section
Arizona Department of Health Services
P.O. Box 3887
Phoenix, AZ 85030
602-255-3260 or 602-364-1300
Fees range from $6 to $9.

Arkansas

Division of Vital Records
Arkansas Department of Health

4815 West Markham Street
Little Rock, AR 72201
501-661-2336
Fees are $4 to $5.

Colorado

Colorado Department of Public Health and
  Environment
4300 Cherry Creek Drive South
HSVRD-VS-AI
Denver, CO 80246-1530
303-756-4464
www.cdphe.state.com.us/hs/cshom.html
Fees are $12 to $15.

Connecticut

Contact the Hall of Records in the town where
  the birth or death occurred.
For marriage or divorce papers, contact the Superior Court office.
Fees are $5.

Delaware

Office of Vital Statistics
Division of Public Health
P.O. Box 637
Dover, DE 19903
302-739-4721 or 302-739-5318
Fees are $2 to $6.

District of Columbia

Vital Records Branch
825 North Capitol Street NE
Washington, DC 20002
202-442-9009
Fees are $12 for birth or death certificates.

Marriage Bureau
515 Fifth Street NW
Washington, DC 20001
Fee is $10 for marriage certificates.

Clerk, Superior Court for the District of Columbia
Family Division
500 Indiana Avenue NW
Washington, DC 20001
Fee is $2 for divorce papers.

Florida

Department of Health and Rehabilitative Services
Office of Vital Statistics
P.O. Box 210
1217 Pearl Street
Jacksonville, FL 32231
904-359-6900
Fees are $5 to $9.

Georgia

Georgia Department of Human Resources
Vital Records Service
Room 217-H
47 Trinity Avenue SW
Atlanta, GA 30334
404-656-4900
www.ph.dhr.statte.ga.us/org/vitalrecords.htm
Fees are $2 to $10.

Guam

Office of Vital Statistics
Department of Public Health and Social Services
Government of Guam
P.O. Box 2816
Agana, GU M.I. 96910
671-734-4589
Fees are $5 and up.

Clerk, Superior Court of Guam
Agana, GU, M.I. 96910
For divorce papers; fees vary

Hawaii

State Department of Health
Office of Health Status Monitoring
Vital Records Section
P.O. Box 3378
Honolulu, HI 96801-9984
808-586-4533
www.Hawaii.gov.health/sdohpg02.htm
Fees are $10 and up.

Idaho

Vital Statistics Unit
Center for Vital Statistics and Health Policy
450 West State Street
First Floor
P.O. Box 8370
Boise, ID 83720-0036
208-334-5988
Fees are $10 and up.

Illinois

Division of Vital Records
Illinois Department of Public Health
605 West Jefferson Street
Springfield, IL 62702-5097
217-782-6553
www.idph.state.il.us
Fees are $5 to $10.

Indiana

Vital Records Section
State Department of Health
2 North Meridian Street
Indianapolis, IN 46204
317-233-2700
Fees are $4 to $6.

Kansas

Office of Vital Statistics
Kansas State Department of Health and Environment

Landon State Office Building
900 SW Jackson Street
Room 151
Topeka, KS 6612-2221
785-296-1400
Fees are $10 and up.

Kentucky

Office of Vital Statistics
Department for Health Services
275 East Main Street
Frankfort, KY 40621
502-564-4212
Fees are $6 to $9.

Louisiana

Vital Records Registry
Office of Public Health
325 Loyola Avenue
New Orleans, LA 70112
504-568-5152
Fees are $5 to $15.

Maine

Office of Vital Statistics
Maine Department of Human Services
State House Station II
Augusta, ME 04333-0011
207-287-3181 (This is a recorded message.)
Fees are $10 and up.

Maryland

Division of Vital Records
Department of Health and Mental Hygiene
6550 Reistertown Avenue
P.O. Box 68760
Baltimore, MD 21215-0020
410-764-3038 or 974-3914
Fees are $6 to $10.

Massachusetts

Registry of Vital Records and Statistics
470 Atlantic Avenue
Second Floor
Boston, MA 02210-2224
617-727-2816
Fees are $3 to $11.

Michigan

Vital Records
3423 North Martin Luther King Boulevard
P.O. Box 30195
Lansing, MI 48909
517-335-8656
www.mdch.state.mi.us/pha/osr
Fee is $13.

Minnesota

Minnesota Department of Health
Section of Vital Statistics
717 Delaware Street, SE

P.O. Box 9441
Minneapolis, MN 55440
612-676-5120
www.health.state.mn.us
Fees are $8 to $14.

Mississippi

Vital Records
State Department of Health
2423 North State Street
Jackson, MS 39216
601-576-7981
Fees are $6 to $12.

Missouri

Missouri Department of Health
Bureau of Vital Records
930 Wildwood
P.O. Box 570
Jefferson City, MO 65102-0570
573-751-6400
www.health.state.mo.us/cgi-bin/uncgi/birthand-
    deathrecords
Fees are $10 and up.

Montana

Montana Department of Public Health and Human
    Services
Vital Statistics Bureau
P.O. Box 4210

Helena, MT 59604
406-444-4228
www.dphhs.state.mt.gov
Fees are $10.

Nebraska

Bureau of Vital Statistics
Department of Health and Human Services
301 Centennial Mall South
P.O. Box 95065
Lincoln, NE 68509-5065
402-471-2871
Fees are $7 to $8.

Nevada

Division of Health—Vital Statistics
Capitol Complex
505 East King Street #102
Carson City, NV 89710
775-684-4280
Fees are $8 to $11.

New Hampshire

Bureau of Vital Records
Health and Welfare Building
6 Hazen Drive
Concord, NH 03301
603-271-4654
Fees are $10.

New Jersey

New Jersey Department of State
Division of Archives and Records Management
P.O. Box 307
Trenton, NJ 08625-0307
609-292-4087
Fee is $4.
For divorce information:
Public Information Center
CN 967
Trenton, NJ 08625
Fee is $10.

New Mexico

Vital Statistics
New Mexico Health Services Division
P.O. Box 26110
Santa Fe, NM 87502
505-827-2338
Fees are $5 to $10.

CLUE: New York City has its own Vital Records Section, separate from the State of New York. For marriage certificate information, contact the city clerk's office in the borough that issued the license if you were a nonresident; or to the borough of the bride's residence (at the time). Richmond is now called Staten Island. You may access information at http://www.nyc.gov/ health or call 212-227-5269.

Write to the City Clerk's Office c/o

Bronx Borough, 1780 Grand Concourse, Bronx, NY 10457

Brooklyn Borough, Municipal Building, Brooklyn, NY 11201

Manhattan Borough, Municipal Building, New York, NY 10007

Queens Borough, 120-55 Queens Boulevard, Kew Gardens, NY 11424

Staten Island, Staten Island Borough Hall, Staten Island, NY 10301

Fee is $10.

For birth, death, or divorce information, contact the state office listed below:

New York City

Division of Vital Records
New York City Department of Health
125 Worth Street
Box 4
New York, NY 10013
212-788-4520 or 212-227-5269
www.nyc.gov/health
Fee is $15.

New York

Certification Unit
Vital Records Section
P.O. Box 2602
Albany, NY 12220-2602
518-474-3075
Fees are $5 to $15.

North Carolina

North Carolina Vital Records
P.O. Box 29537
Raleigh, NC 27626-0537
919-733-3526
www.schs.state.nc.us.SCHS/
Fee is $10.

North Dakota

Division of Vital Records
State Capitol
600 East Boulevard Avenue
Bismarck, ND 58505-0200
701-328-2360
www.health.state.nd.us
Records can be ordered online.
Fees are $5 to $7.

Northern Mariana Islands

Superior Court
Vital Records Section
P.O. Box 307
Saipan, MP 96950
670-234-6401, ext. 15
Fees are $3.

CLUE: Years from 1945 to 1950 are incomplete.

Ohio

Bureau of Vital Statistics
Ohio Department of Health
P.O. Box 15098
Columbus, OH 43215-0098
614-486-2531
Fee is $7.

Oklahoma

Vital Records Section
State Department of Health
1000 Northeast 10th Street
P.O. Box 53551
Oklahoma City, OK 73152
405-271-4040
Fees are $5 to $10.

Oregon

Oregon Health Division
Vital Statistics Section
P.O. Box 14050
Portland, OR 97293-0050
503-731-4095
www.ohd.hr.state.or.us
Fees are $15.

Pennsylvania

Division of Vital Records
State Department of Health
Central Building

101 South Mercer Street
P.O. Box 1528
New Castle, PA 16103
724-656-3100
Fees are $3 to $5.

Puerto Rico

Department of Health
Demographic Registry
P.O. Box 11854
Fernandez Juncos Station
San Juan, PR 00910
(787) 728-7980
Fees are $2 each.

CLUE: Information from July 22, 1931, only.

Rhode Island

Division of Vital Records
Rhode Island Department of Health
3 Capitol Hill
Room 101
Providence, RI 02908-5095
401-222-2811
Fee is $15.

For divorce papers:
Clerk of Family Court
One Dorrance Plaza
Providence, RI 02903
Fee is $3.

South Carolina

Office of Public Health Statistics and Information Systems
South Carolina Department of Health and Environmental Control
2600 Bull Street
Columbia, SC 29201
803-898-3630
Fee is $12.

South Dakota

Vital Records
State Department of Health
600 East Capitol Avenue
Pierre, SD 57501-2536
605-773-3355
www.state.sd.us/doh/vitalrec/vital.htm
Fee is $7.

Tennessee

Tennessee Vital Records
Department of Health
Central Services Building
421 Fifth Avenue North
Nashville, TN 37247-0450
615-741-1763
www.state.tn.us/health/vr/index.htm
Fees are $5 to $10.

Texas

Bureau of Vital Statistics
Texas Department of Health
P.O. Box 12040
Austin, TX 78711-2040
512-458-7111
www.tdh.state.tx.us/bvs
Fees are $9 to $11.

Utah

Utah Department of Health
288 North 1460 West
P.O. Box 141012
Salt Lake City, UT 84114-1012
801-538-6105
Note: Marriage and divorce records date only to 1978.
hlunix.hlx.state.ut.us/bvr/html/vital_statistics.html
Fee is $9 to 12.

Vermont

Vermont Department of Health
Vital Records Section
P.O. Box 70
108 Cherry Street
Burlington, VT 05402
802-828-3286
Fee is $7.

Virgin Islands

Registrar of Vital Statistics for Birth or Death in
St. Croix
Charles Harwood Memorial Hospital
Christiansted
St. Croix, VI 00820

Registrar of Vital Statistics for Birth or Death in
St. Thomas and St. John
Knud Hansen Complex
Hospital Ground
Charlotte Amalie
St. Thomas, VI 00802

For marriage or divorce:
Bureau of Vital Records and Statistical Services
Virgin Islands Department of Health
Charlotte Amalie
St. Thomas, VI 00801

Chief Deputy Clerk
Family Division
Territorial Court of the Virgin Islands
P.O. Box 929
Christiansted
St. Croix, VI 00820

For St. Thomas and St. John:
Clerk of the Territorial Court of the Virgin Islands
Family Division
P.O. Box 70
Charlotte Amalie
St. Croix, VI 00801

Telephone number is the same for all islands:
340-774-9000, ext. 4621 or 4623
Fees are $2 to $15.

Virginia

Office of Vital Records and Health Statistics
State Health Department
P.O. Box 1000
Richmond, VA 3218-1000
804-225-5000
Fee is $8.

Washington

Department of Health
Center for Health Statistics
P.O. Box 9709
Olympia, WA 98507-9709
360-236-4300
wxk0303@hub.doh.wa.gov
Fees range from $13 and up.

West Virginia

Vital Registration Office
Division of Health
State Capitol Complex, Building 3
Charleston, WV 25305
304-558-2931
No Web site at press time
Fees range from $5 and up.

Wisconsin

Vital Records
One West Wilson Street
P.O. Box 309
Madison, WI 53701
608-266-1371
www.dhfs.state.wi.us/vitalrecords/vitlindex.htm
Fees range from $7 to $12.

Wyoming

Vital Records Services
Hathaway Building
Cheyenne, WY 82002
307-777-7591
http:wdhfs.state.wy.us/vital_records
Fees are $9 to $12.

Appendix II

SOCIAL SECURITY CONGRESSIONAL COMMITTEE MEMBERS

Your Congressional representatives and Senators represent *you*.

If you have concerns about the laws that govern the Social Security Administration (which administrates the laws; it doesn't make them), *write* or *call* your Congressional representatives in Washington, D.C., and their local district offices.

District phone numbers are listed below for your convenience. Don't be frustrated if the number you reach is a voice mail; calls will be returned. Supplement this call by writing via e-mail or U.S. mail.

Changes occur when the public protests. It's your *right* and your *privilege*.

All these names were accurate at press time; however, committee membership can be altered at any time when elected officials choose to retire, change their congressional committee status, or die while in office.

President George W. Bush

The White House

1600 Pennsylvania Avenue NW

Washington, D.C. 20500

The White House switchboard: 202-456-1414

The White House fax number: 202-456-2461

The White House TTY/TDD phone number for the hearing impaired only comment line: 202-456-6213

e-mail: president@whitehouse.gov

Vice President Dick Cheney: vice.president@whitehouse.gov

Congress has two houses, the Senate and the House of Representatives. Each house has committees and/or subcommittees on health, aging, and Social Security, with majority and minority party leadership for each. All of these committees influence and are influenced by matters handled by Social Security.

Although e-mail correspondence is easiest, sometimes that path is overloaded. Make calls or write to the local offices first in your district or state, then contact your representatives' Washington office. The chances for direct communication are always easier on the local level, although some of them receive so many calls they use voice mail to accommodate them. Don't let that frustrate you. Call, write, e-mail, fax, or do whatever you need to so they listen to your concerns. Committee chairs and members are subject to change at any time.

Senate Subcommittee on Social Security and Family Policy

202-224-4515 (Majority)
202-224-7800 (Minority)
Fax: Not available

Address: 219 Dirksen Senate Office Building, Washington, D.C. 20510 (Majority)
203 Hart Senate Office Building, Washington, D.C. 20510 (Minority)

District phone numbers are listed first, then Washington numbers. *Note:* Some representatives serve on more than one committee; they are all listed.

Senate Majority Party Members

Sen. John Breaux (D-LA), 504-589-2531,
    district; 202-224-4623, D.C.
senator@breaux.senate.gov

Sen. Jim Jeffords (I-VT), 802-658-6001, district; 202-224-5141, D.C.
vermont@jeffords.senate.gov

Sen. Jay Rockefeller (D-WV)
304-347-537, district; 202-224-6472, D.C.
senator@rockefeller.senate.gov

Sen. Charles Schumer (D-NY), 212-486-4430, district;
    202-224-6542, D.C.
senator@schumer.senate.gov

Senate Minority Party Members

Sen. Phil Gramm (R-TX), 214-767-3000,
   district; 202-224-2934, D.C.
   Phil_Gramm@gramm.senate.gov

Sen. Trent Lott (R-MS), 601-965-4644,
   district; 202-224-6253, D.C.
   senatorlott@lott.senate.gov

Sen. Don Nickles (R-OK), 405-231-4941,
   district; 202-224-5754, D.C.
   senator@nickles.senate.gov

Sen. Fred Thompson (R-TN), 615-736-5129,
   district; 202-224-4944, D.C.
   senator_thompson@thompson. senate.gov

Subcommittee on Social Security

202-225-9263 (Majority)
202-225-9263 (Minority)

Fax:
202-225-9480 (Majority)
202-225-9480 (Minority)

Address:
B-316 Rayburn House Office Building, Washington,
   D.C. 20515 (Majority)
1106 Longworth House Office Building, Washington,
   D.C. 20515 (Minority)

Parent Committee: House Committee on Ways and Means House Majority Party Members

Kevin Brady (R-TX), 281-895-8892,
  district; 202-225-4901, D.C.
  rep.brady@mail.house.gov

Mac Collins (R-GA), 770-603-3395,
  district; 202-225-5901, D.C.
  mac.collins@mail.house.gov

J. D. Hayworth (R-AZ), 602-926-4151,
  district; 202-225-2190, D.C.
  jdhayworth@mail.house.gov

Kenny C. Hulshof (R-MO), 573-449-5111,
  district; 202-225-2956, D.C.
  rep.hulshof@mail.house.gov

Sam Johnson (R-TX), 214-739-0182,
  district; 202-225-4201, D.C.
  http://wwwa.house.gov/samjohnson/IMA/get_address.htm

Ron Lewis (R-KY), 270-842-9896,
  district; 202-225-3501, D.C.
  ron.lewis@mail.house.gov

Paul Ryan (R-WI), 608-752-4050,
  district; 202-225-3031, D.C.
  http://www.house.gov/ryan/emailzipcheck. html

E. Clay Shaw, Jr. (R-FL), 954-522-1800,
  district; 202-225-3026, D.C.
  http://www.house.gov/writerep/

House Minority Party Members

Xavier Becerra (D-CA), 213-483-1425,
district; 202-225-6235, D.C.
http://www.house.gov/writerep/

Benjamin L. Cardin (D-MD), 410-433-8886,
district; 202-225-4016, D.C.
rep.cardin@mail.house.gov

Lloyd Doggett (D-TX), 512-916-5921,
district; 202-225-4865, D.C.
lloyd.doggett@mail.house.gov

Robert T. Matsui (D-CA), 916-498-5600,
district; 202-225-7163, D.C.
http://www.house.gov/writerep/

Earl Pomeroy (D-ND), 701-224-0355,
district; 202-225-2611, D.C.
Rep.Earl.Pomeroy@mail.house.gov

Subcommittee on Aging

202-224-0136 (Majority)
202-224-3239 (Minority)

Fax:
202-228-0581 (Majority)
202-228-0404 (Minority)

Address:
615 Hart Senate Office Building, Washington, D.C.
20510 (Majority)

113 Hart Senate Office Building, Washington, D.C. 20510 (Minority)

Senate Majority Party Members

Sen. Christopher Dodd (D-CT), 860-240-3470,
   district; 202-224-2823, D.C.
senator@dodd.senate.gov

Sen. Jim Jeffords (I-VT), 802-658-6001,
   district; 202-224-5141, D.C.
vermont@jeffords.senate.gov

Sen. Barbara Mikulski (D-MD), 410-263-1805,
   district; 202-224-4654, D.C.
senator@mikulski.senate.gov

Senate Minority Party Members

Sen. Mike DeWine (R-OH), 614-469-5186,
   district; 202-224-2315, D.C.
senator_dewine@dewine.senate.gov

Sen. Judd Gregg (R-NH), 603-225-7115,
   district; 202-224-3324, D.C.
mailbox@gregg.senate.gov

Sen. Tim Hutchinson (R-AR), 501-324-6336,
   district; 202-224-2353, D.C.
Senator.Hutchinson@hutchinson.senate.gov

Senate Committee on Health, Education, Labor, and Pensions

202-224-5375 (Majority)
202-224-5465 (Minority)

Fax:
202-224-6510 (Majority)
202-224-5128 (Minority)

Address:
428 Dirksen Senate Office Building, Washington, D.C. 20510 (Majority)
646 Dirksen Senate Office Building, Washington, D.C. 20510 (Minority)

Senate Majority Party Members

Sen. Jeff Bingaman (D-NM), 505-988-6647, district; 202-224-5521, D.C.
Senator_Bingaman@bingaman. senate.gov

Sen. Christopher Dodd (D-CT), 860-240-3470, district; 202-224-2823, D.C.
senator@dodd.senate.gov

Sen. Tom Harkin (D-IA), 515-284-4574, district; 202-224-3254, D.C.
tom_harkin@harkin.senate.gov

Sen. Jim Jeffords (I-VT), 802-658-6001, district; 202-224-5141, D.C.
vermont@jeffords.senate.gov

Sen. Edward M. Kennedy (D-MA), 617-565-3170,
   district; 202-224-4543, D.C.
senator@kennedy.senate.gov

Sen. Barbara Mikulski (D-MD), 410-263-1805,
   district; 202-224-4654, D.C.
senator@mikulski.senate.gov

Sen. John F. "Jack" Reed (D-RI), 401-943-3100,
   district; 202-224-4642, D.C.
jack@reed.senate.gov

Sen. Paul David Wellstone (D-MN), 651-645-0323,
   district; 202-224-5641, D.C.
http://wellstone.senate.gov/webform.html

Senate Minority Party Members

Sen. Sam Brownback (R-KS), 913-492-6378,
   district; 202-224-6521, D.C.
webmail@brownback.senate.gov

Sen. Susan M. Collins (R-ME), 207-945-0417,
   district; 202-224-2523, D.C.
senator@collins.senate.gov

Sen. Mike DeWine (R-OH), 614-469-5186,
   district; 202-224-2315, D.C.
senator_dewine@dewine.senate.gov

Sen. Michael Enzi (R-WY), 307-261-6572,
   district; 202-224-3424, D.C.
senator@enzi.senate.gov

Sen. Bill Frist (R-TN), 615-352-9411,
    district; 202-224-3344, D.C.
senator_frist@frist.senate.gov

Sen. Judd Gregg (R-NH), 603-225-7115,
    district; 202-224-3324, D.C.
mailbox@gregg.senate.gov

Sen. Tim Hutchinson (R-AR), 501-324-6336,
    district; 202-224-2353, D.C.
Senator.Hutchinson@hutchinson.senate.gov

Sen. Jeff Sessions (R-AL), 205-731-1500,
    district; 202-224-4124, D.C.
senator@sessions.senate.gov

Appendix III

GLOSSARY OF
SOCIAL SECURITY TERMS

AIME (Average Indexed Monthly Earnings). The dollar amount used to calculate your Social Security benefit after 1978 when you become age 62 or disabled (or die). To arrive at your AIME, the SSA will adjust your actual past earnings using an "average wage index," so you won't lose the value of your past earnings (when money was worth more) in relation to your more recent earnings. If you became age 62 or became disabled (or died) before 1978, the SSA used the **Average Monthly Earnings (AME).** For more information online, go to www.ssa.gov/OP_Home/handbook/handbook.07/handbook-0701.html.

AME (Average Monthly Earnings). The dollar amount used in calculating your monthly Social Security benefit if you were age 62 or became disabled (or died) before 1978. The AME is determined by dividing the total earnings in the "computation years" by the number of months in those same years. For more information, go to www.ssa.gov/OP_Home/handbook/handbook.07/handbook-0701.html.

Appeal (Appeal Rights). Whenever Social Security makes a decision that affects your eligibility for Social Security or Supplemental Security Income benefits, they will send you a letter explaining the decision. If you disagree with the decision, you have a right to appeal it. If the decision is demonstrated to be wrong, the SSA will change it.

Application for Benefits. To receive Social Security or Black Lung benefits, Supplemental Security Income payments, or Medicare, you must complete and sign an application. You can apply for retirement benefits and spouse's benefits online at www.ssa.gov/applytoretire, in person at any SSA office, or by telephone at 800-772-1213. The deaf or hard of hearing may call the TTY number, 800-325-0778. For information online for other services, go to www.ssa.gov/howto.htm.

Baptismal Certificate. A religious record of your birth or baptism. In some situations, the SSA will use a baptismal certificate to establish your age. For more information, go to www.ssa.gov/OP_Home/handbook/handbook.17/handbook-1700.html.

Base Years. For computing Social Security benefits, the years after 1950 up to the year you're entitled to retirement or disability insurance benefits are referred to as the base years. For a survivor's claim, the base years include the year of the worker's death. See **RIB (Retirement Insurance Benefit).** For more information online, go to www.ssa.gov/OP_Home/handbook/handbook.07/handbook-0701.html.

Benefits. Social Security provides five major categories of benefits: retirement, disability, family (dependents), survivors, and Medicare. The retirement, disability, family (dependents), and survivors programs provide monthly cash benefits. Medicare provides medical coverage.

Benefits (Reduced). You can get the following reduced monthly benefits *before* reaching full retirement age:

1. retirement insurance benefits at age 62 through the month before you reach **(FRA) Full Retirement Age**
2. husband's or wife's insurance benefits at age 62 through the month before you reach FRA, provided no child of your spouse either under age 18 or disabled and entitled to benefits is in your care
3. widow(er) insurance benefits beginning at any time from age 50 through the month before you reach FRA
4. widow(er) insurance benefits after your spouse has received a retirement insurance benefit reduced for age
5. disability insurance benefits received after a reduced retirement insurance benefit or retirement or disability insurance benefit received after a reduced widow(er) insurance benefit. (This applies only if you were born before 1928.)

Benefit Verification Letter (BEVE). An official letter from the SSA that provides information on how much you receive in monthly Social Security benefits and/or Supplemental Security Income payments. To receive this letter, you or your authorized representative must request it.

Birth Certificate. The record maintained by a government entity such as a state, county, parish, city, or borough, which documents your birth. *Note:* In some cases a baptismal certificate may be acceptable; always ask. For more information online, see *How to Write for Vital Records* at www.ssa.gov/vitalstats.html.

Child. The term used to include your biological child or any other child who can inherit your personal property under state law or who meets certain specific requirements under the Social Security Act, such as a legally adopted child or an equitably adopted child, stepchild, or grandchild.

COLA (Cost of Living Adjustments). Social Security benefits and Supplemental Security Income payments are increased each year to keep pace with increases in the cost-of-living (inflation).

Computation Years. The years with highest earnings selected from the "base years." The SSA adds the total earnings in the computation years and divides by the number of months in those years to get the AIME or the AME, using your highest 35 years of earnings to compute your retirement benefits.

CPI-W (Consumer Price Index). An index prepared by the U.S. Department of Labor that charts the rise in costs for selected goods and services. This index is used to compute **COLA (Cost of Living Adjustments).**

Credits (Social Security Credits). As you work and pay taxes, you earn credits that count toward your eligibility for future Social Security benefits. You can earn a maximum of 4 credits each year. Most people need 40 credits to qualify for benefits. Younger people need fewer credits to qualify for disability or survivors benefits. Previously called **QC (Quarters of Coverage).** For more information online, see *How You Earn Credits* at www.ssa.gov/pubs/10072.html.

Decision Notice (Award Letter or Denial Letter). When you file for Social Security, the SSA decides if and when you will receive benefits. They will send you an official letter explaining their decision, and if benefits are available, they will tell you how much you will receive in an Award Letter. If they determine you are ineligible, they will send you a Denial Letter that can be appealed. **See Appeal (Appeal Rights).**

Direct Deposit. The standard way to receive Social Security benefits and Supplemental Security Income payments. Your money is sent electronically to an account in a financial institution (a bank, trust company, savings and loan association, brokerage agency, or credit union). For more information online, go to *Direct Deposit of Benefits* at www.ssa.gov/deposit/.

Disability Benefits. You can get disability benefits if you are under full retirement age, have enough Social Security credits and a severe medical impairment (physical or mental) that's expected to prevent you from doing "substantial" work for a year or more, or have a condition that is expected to result in death. For more information online, go to *Disability Programs* at www.ssa.gov/disability/.

Documents or **"Proofs."** Forms and papers such as birth certificates, marriage certificates, W-2 Forms, tax returns, deeds, etc., submitted by individuals applying for benefits and services. Only originals or copies certified by the agency that has the original document are acceptable. (See **Evidence or "Proofs"**). For more information online go to www.ssa.gov/OP_Home/handbook/handbook.17/handbook-toc17.html.

DRC (Delayed Retirement Credit). The SSA increases your benefits by a certain percentage, depending upon your date of birth, if you delay your retirement beyond the full retirement age. Increases based on delaying retirement no longer apply when you reach age 70, even if you continue to delay taking benefits.

Early Retirement. You can receive Social Security retirement benefits as early as age 62, but your benefit amount will be less than you would have gotten at full retirement age. If you take retirement benefits early, your benefit will be permanently reduced, based on the number of months you received checks before you reached full retirement age. See **RIB (Retirement Insurance Benefits).** For more information online, go to www.ssa.gov/retirement/.

Earnings Record. The chronological history of the amount you earn each year during your working lifetime. The credits you earned remain on your Social Security record even when you change jobs or have no earnings.

Evidence or "Proofs." Documents you must submit to support a factor of entitlement or payment amount. The Social Security office can explain what evidence is required to establish entitlement and help you to get it.

Family Benefits (Dependent Benefits). When you're eligible for retirement or disability benefits, the following people may receive benefits on your record:

1. a spouse, if he or she is at least 62 years old (or any age but caring for an entitled child under age 16)
2. children, if they are unmarried and under age 18, under 19, and a full-time elementary or secondary student
3. children age 18 or older but disabled
4. divorced ex-spouse

Family Maximum. The maximum amount of benefits payable to an entire family on any one worker's record.

FICA Tax. The amount withheld from your salary or self-employment income that funds the Social Security and

Medicare programs. FICA is an abbreviation for the Federal Insurance Contributions Act that made it legal to put this tax on your income/earnings from employment.

Food Stamps. The U.S. Department of Agriculture Food Stamp Program helps needy families to buy food. It is not part of the Social Security Administration, but many beneficiaries of SSA benefits may also qualify for food stamps. For more information read the brochure *Food Stamps and Other Nutrition Programs,* or go to more information online at www.ssa.gov/pubs/10100.html.

FRA (Full Retirement Age). The age at which you may first become entitled to unreduced retirement benefits. Beginning with the year 2000, the retirement age of a worker or spouse born 1938 or later, or a widow(er) born 1940 or later, began to increase gradually from age 65. Retirement age reached age 67 in the year 2002. The higher FRA affects your benefit amount if you choose to receive reduced benefits.

Health Insurance (Medicare). The federal health insurance program for: people 65 years of age or older; people with permanent kidney failure who use dialysis or acquire a transplant (sometimes called ESRD or end-stage renal disease); and certain younger people with disabilities. Medicare generally covers health plans, nursing homes, dialysis facilities, Medigap policies, Medicare activities, participating physicians, and prescription drugs. For more information online, access www.hcfa.gov/medicaid/medicaid.htm.

Insured Status. If you earned enough Social Security credits to meet the eligibility requirement for retirement (40) or the variable amount of credits needed to receive disability benefits or enable your dependents to establish eligibility for benefits owing to your retirement, disability, or death, you have insured status. For more information online, access *Credits* on www.ssa.gov/pubs/10072.html.

Lawful Alien Status. A person achieves lawful alien status if he or she has been admitted to the United States and granted permanent authorization to work by the Immigration and Nationalization Service (INS), or if the person is admitted to the United States on a temporary basis with INS authorization to work.

Lifetime Earnings. See **Earnings Record.**

Lump Sum Death Payment. A one-time payment of $255, paid in addition to any monthly survivors' insurance benefits that are due. This benefit is paid only to your widow(er) or minor children.

Marriage. Generally, the term "marriage" applies to SSA issues only to marriages between men and women who have obtained certificates and licenses from the community. Homosexual or common law marriages are still not recognized by the Social Security Administration. Although some religions accept multiple marriages, bigamy can lead to the loss of Social Security benefits of surviving spouses.

Maximum Earnings. The maximum earnings counted for any calendar year when computing your Social Security benefits.

Medicaid. A joint federal and state program that helps with medical costs for people with low incomes and limited resources. Medicaid programs vary from state to state, but most healthcare costs are covered if you qualify for both Medicare and Medicaid. For more information, access www.hcfa.gov/medicaid/medicaid.htm.

Medicare. See **Health Insurance (Medicare).**

MOE (Month of Election). Usually applies to retirement claims. In certain situations, you can choose the month in which your benefits will start. Your local SSA office can help you decide which month is best for you to earn the most from your benefits.

NH (Number Holder). See **Wage Earner.**

OASDI (Old Age Survivors and Disability Insurance). The Social Security programs that provide monthly cash benefits to you and your dependents when you retire, to your surviving dependents, and to disabled workers and their dependents.

Payment Dates for Social Security Benefits. If you filed for Social Security benefits before May 1, 1997, your payments usually are dated and delivered on the third of the month following the month for which the payment is due. For example, payments for January are delivered on February third. If the third of the month is a Saturday, Sunday, or federal holiday, your payments are dated and delivered on the first day before the third of the month that is not a Saturday, Sunday, or federal holiday. For example, if the third is a Saturday or Sunday, payments are delivered on the preceding Friday.

If you filed for Social Security benefits May 1, 1997, or later, you are assigned one of three new payment days based on the date of birth of the insured person: If you were born on the first through the tenth of the month, your payment will be delivered on the second Wednesday of the month; if you were born on the eleventh through twentieth of the month, your check will be dated the third Wednesday of the month; if you were born on the twenty-first through the end of the month, your check will be delivered on the fourth Wednesday of the month.

If your scheduled Wednesday payment day is a federal holiday, your payment will be sent on the preceding day that is not a federal legal holiday.

SSI payments are usually dated and delivered on the first of the month for which they are due. However, if the first falls on a Saturday, Sunday, or federal holiday, the SSA dates and sends them on the first day preceding the first of the month that is not a Saturday, Sunday, or federal holiday. For more information online about the payment calendar, access www.ssa.gov/pubs/2001calendar. htm.

PIA (Primary Insurance Amount). The monthly amount payable if you are a retired worker who begins receiving benefits at full retirement age, or if you're disabled and have never received a retirement benefit reduced for age.

Proofs. See **Documents or "Proofs"** and **Evidence or "Proofs."**

Protective Filing Date. The date you first contact the SSA to file for benefits.

QC (Quarters of Coverage). Social Security credits. As you work and pay taxes, you earn credits that count toward eligibility for future Social Security benefits. You can earn a maximum of 4 credits each year and most people need 40 credits to qualify for benefits. Younger people need fewer credits to qualify for disability or for their spouse or children to qualify for survivors benefits. During their working lifetime most workers earn more credits than needed to be eligible for Social Security. These extra credits do not increase eventual Social Security benefits. However, the income earned may increase the benefit amount. For more information online, read *How You Earn Credits* at www.ssa.gov/pubs/10072.html.

Record of Earnings. See **Earnings Record.**

Reduction Months. This is the period of time beginning with the first month you're entitled to reduced benefits up to, but not including, the month in which you reach full retirement age.

Representative Payee. If you receive Social Security benefits or Supplemental Security Income and become unable to handle your own financial affairs, after a careful investigation you will be appointed an interested party to handle your Social Security matters. This can be a relative, friend, or a social worker. Representative payees are required to maintain complete accounting records and periodically provide reports to Social Security. For additional information online read *Representative Payment Program* at www.ssa.gov/payee/.

Retirement Age (Full). Full retirement age was 65 for many years. However, beginning with the year 2000, the retirement age for workers and spouses born 1938 or later, or widows(ers) born 1940 or later increased gradually from age 65 until it reached age 67 in the year 2002.

Retirement Age (Minimum). The minimum age for retirement is age 62 for workers and age 50 for widow(er)s.

You can choose a reduced benefit anytime between the minimum ages and your full retirement age; however, it will always be lower than the full benefit.

Retirement Earnings Test. If you get Social Security benefits, are under full retirement age, and work, your earnings from wages and/or self-employment that exceed a certain maximum will cause a deduction in your monthly benefits. For more information online, access *How Work Affects Your Benefits* at www.ssa.gov/pubs/10069.html.

Retroactive Benefits "Back Pay." Monthly benefits that you may be entitled to before the month you actually file an application, if you meet the entitlement requirements.

RIB (Retirement Insurance Benefits). Money that is payable to you at full retirement age (you can get reduced benefits as early as age 62) if you have enough Social Security credits. For more information online, go to www.ssa.gov/retirement/.

SEI (Self-Employment Income). If you operate a trade, business, or profession as an individual or with a partner, and you have net earnings of $400 or more in a taxable year, you are considered self-employed. For more information online, read *If You're Self-Employed* on www.ssa.gov/pubs/10022.html.

Social Security. While you work, you pay taxes into the Social Security system, and when you retire or become disabled, you, your spouse, and your dependent children receive monthly benefits that are based on your reported earnings. In addition, your survivors can collect benefits when you die. For more information online, read *Social Security, A Snapshot* on www.ssa.gov/pubs/10006.html.

Social Security Number (SSN). Your first and continuous link with Social Security is your nine-digit Social Security Number (SSN). Your SSN helps the SSA to maintain an accurate record of your wages or self-employment earnings covered under the Social Security Act. The SSN is also the link to monitoring your benefits when you begin earning them.

Social Security Office. The SSA maintains more than 1300 offices throughout the country. Your local Social Security office is the place where you can:

1. Apply for a Social Security number (SSN).
2. Check on your earnings record, and apply for Social Security benefits, black lung benefits, Supplemental Security Income (SSI), or hospital insurance protection (Medicare).
3. Enroll for medical insurance.
4. Get help with applying for food stamps.
5. Learn everything you need to know about your rights and obligations under the Social Security law.

Spouse. You are considered the spouse of a worker when he or she applied for benefits if you and the worker were validly married, you would have the status of a husband or a wife for that person's personal property if they had no will, or you went through a marriage ceremony in good faith, which would have been valid except for a legal impediment.

SS-5. The application form you need to get a Social Security number, a replacement card, or a duplicate card. For more information online, access www.ssa.gov/ss-5.html.

SSI (Supplemental Security Income). The SSI is a federal supplemental income program funded by general tax revenues (not Social Security taxes). It helps aged, blind, and disabled people who have little or no income by providing monthly cash payments to meet basic needs for food, clothing, and shelter. For more information online, access *Supplemental Security Income* at www.ssa.gov/notices/supplemental-security-income/.

Survivor (Survivors Benefits). Payments based on your record (if you should die) are paid to:

1. Your widow(er) age 60 or older, 50 or older if disabled, or any age if caring for a child under age 16 or who became disabled before age 22.
2. Your children, if they are unmarried and under age 18, under 19 but still in school, or 18 or older but disabled before age 22.
3. Your parents, if you provided at least one-half of their support.
4. Your ex-spouse, who could be eligible for a widow(er)'s benefit on your record.

A special one-time, lump sum payment of $255 may also be made to your widow(er) or minor children.

For more information online, access *Survivors Benefits* at www.ssa.gov/pubs/deathbenefits.htm.

Wage Earner. A person who earns Social Security credits while working for wages or self-employment income. Sometimes referred to as a number holder or worker.

Wages. All payment for services performed for an employer. Wages don't have to be cash. The cash value of all compensation paid to an employee in any form other than cash is also considered wages (unless the form of payment is specifically not covered under the Social Security Act).

Widow(er). You are the widow(er) of the insured person if, at the time the insured person died, you and the insured person were validly married, you would have the status of a husband or a wife for that person's personal property if the person had no will, or you went through a marriage ceremony in good faith that would have been valid except for a legal impediment.

Work Credits. See **Credits (Social Security Credits)** and **(QC) Quarters of Coverage.**

Worker. See **Wage Earner.**

Appendix IV
PRINT PUBLICATIONS

CLUE: You can read more about any segment or program of the Social Security Administration *free* in these and many other publications. Most, but not all, are available in print in English and in Spanish. Some publications are available in other languages.

The Future of Social Security
Publication No. 05-100055
www.ssa.gov/pubs/10055/html
En Español: Publication No. 05-10955
www.ssa.gov/Espanol/10955.html

Schedule of Social Security Benefit Payments
Publication No. 05-10031
www.ssa.gov/pubs/10031.html
En Español: Publication No. 05-10931
www.ssa.gov/Espanol/10931.html

Social Security: A "Snapshot"
Publication No. 05-10006
www.ssa.gov/pubs/10006.html

En Español: Publication No. 05-10906
www.ssa.gov/Espanol/10906.html

Social Security: How You Earn Credits
Publication No. 05-10072
www.ssa.gov/pubs/10072.html
En Español: Publication No. 05-10972
www.ssa.gov/Espanol/10972.html

Social Security Basic Facts
Publication No. 05-10080
www.ssa.gov/pubs/10080.html
En Español: Publication No. 05-10980
www.ssa.gov/Espanol/10980.html

Social Security: Understanding the Benefits
Publication No. 05-10024
www.ssa.gov/pubs/10024
En Español: Publication No. 05-10924
www.ssa.gov/Espanol/10924.html

Social Security: What Every Woman Should Know
Publication No. 05-10127
www.ssa.gov/pubs/10127.html

Disability
Publication No. 05-10029
www.ssa.gov/pubs/10029
En Español: Publication No. 05-10929
www.ssa.gov/Espanol/10929.html

The Appeals Process
Publication No. 05-10141
www.ssa.gov/pubs.10141.html

Disability Evaluation Under Social Security—The Blue Book
64-039

*A Guide to Social Security and SSI Disability Benefits for
People with HIV Infection*
Publication No. 05-10020
www.ssa.gov/pubs/10020.html
En Español: Publication No. 05-10920
www.ssa.gov/Espanol/10920.html

How We Decide If You Are Still Disabled
Publication No. 05-10053
www.ssa.gov/pubs/10053.html

*How Worker's Compensation and Other Disability Payments
May Affect Your Benefits*
Publication No. 05-10018
www.ssa.gov/pubs/10018.html

Receive Your Benefits by Direct Deposit
Publication No. 05-10123
www.ssa.gov/pubs/10123.html.
En Español: Reciba Sus Beneficios Por Depósito Directo
Publication No. 05-10923

Reviewing Your Disability
Publication No. 05-10068
www.ssa.gov/pubs/10068.html
En Español: Publication No. 05-10968
www.ssa.gov/Espanol/l0968.html

Social Security: Benefits for Children with Disabilities
Publication No. 05-10026

www.ssa.gov/pubs/10026.html
En Español: Publication No. 05-10926
www.ssa.gov/espanol/10926.html

Social Security: If You Are Blind How We Can Help
Publication No. 05-10052
www.ssa.gov/pubs/10052.html

Social Security: What You Need to Know When You Get Disability Benefits
Publication No. 05-10153
www.ssa.gov/pubs/10153.html
En Español: Publication No. 05-10903
www.ssa.gov/espanol/10903.html

Social Security Benefits for People Living with HIV/AIDS
Publication No. 05-10019

Ticket to Work and Work Incentives Improvement Act of 1999
Publication No. 05-10060

Working While Disabled . . . How We Can Help
Publication No. 05-10095
En Español: Publication No. 05-10995

Retirement Benefits
Publication No. 05-10035
En Español: Publication No. 05-10935

How Work Affects Your Benefits
Publication No. 05-10069
En Español: Publication No. 05-10969

The Notch: What It Is . . . And What It Isn't
Publication No. 05-10042

Receive Your Benefits by Direct Deposit
Publication No. 05-10123
En Español: Publication No. 05-10123

Social Security: What You Need to Know When You Get
*   Retirement or Survivors Benefits*
Publication No. 05-10077
En Español: Publication No. 05-10977

Special Payments After Retirement
Publication No. 05-10063 0

Survivors
Publication No. 05-10084
En Español: Publication No. 05-10984

Supplemental Security Income
Publication No. 05-11000
En Español: Publication No. 05-11090

The Definition of Disability for Children
Publication No. 05-11053
En Español: Publication No. 05-11054

A Guide to Social Security and SSI Disability Benefits for
*   People with HIV Infection*
Publication No. 05-10020
En Español: Publication No. 05-10920

How Worker's Compensation and Other Disability Payments May Affect Your Benefits
Publication No. 05-10018

Receiving Your Benefits by Direct Deposit
Publication No. 05-10123
En Español: Publication No. 05-10923

Reviewing Your Disability
Publication No. 05-10068
En Español: Publication No. 05-10968

Social Security: What You Need to Know When You Get SSI 1
Publication No. 05-11011
En Español: Publication No. 05-11024

Social Security: Working While Disabled . . . A Guide to Plans for Achieving Self-Support PASS
Publication No. 05-11017
En Español: Publication No. 05-10997

Social Security: You May Be Able to Get SSI
Publication No. 05-11069

Special Benefits for Certain World War II Veterans
Factsheet Publication No. 05-10157
Booklet Publication No. 05-10158

Supplemental Security Income for Noncitizens
Publication No. 05-11051
En Español: Publication No. 05-11052

Your Right to Question the Decision Made on Your SSI Claim
Publication No. 05-11008
En Español: Publication No. 05-11098

Appeals
Publication No. 05-10041
En Español: Publication No. 05-10941

The Appeals Process
Publication No. 05-10141

How to File an Unfair Treatment Complaint
Publication No. 05-10071

Your Right to Representation
Publication No. 05-10075
En Español: Publication No. 05-10975

Your Right to Question the Decision Made on Your Claim
Publication No. 05-10058
En Español: Publication No. 05-10958

*Your Right to Question the Decision Made on Your SSI
     Claim*
Publication No. 05-11008
En Español: Publication No. 05-11098

Changing Your Name?
Publication No. 05-10642

*When You Need a Social Security Number and When You
     Don't*
Publication No. 05-10096
En Español: Publication No. 05-10996

Social Security: Numbers for Children
Publication No. 05-10023
www.ssa.gov/pubs/10023.html
En Español: Publication No. 05-10923
www.ssa.gov/espanol/10923.html

When Someone Misuses Your Social Security Number
Publication No. 05-10064
www.ssa.gov/pubs/10064.html
En Español: Publication No. 05-10964
www.ssa.gov/Espanol/10964.html

How State and Local Government Employees Are Covered by
    Social Security and Medicare
Publication No. 05-10051

A Guide for Farmers Growers and Crew Leaders
Publication No. 05-10025
En Español: Publication No. 05-10925

Household Workers
Publication No. 05-10021
En Español: Publication No. 05-10922

How International Agreements Can Help You
Publication No. 05-10180

How Work Affects Your Benefits
Publication No. 05-10069
En Español: Publication No. 05-10969

If You Are Self-Employed
Publication No. 05-10022
En Español: Publication No. 05-10922

If You Work for a Nonprofit Organization
Publication No. 05-10027
En Español: Publication No. 05-10927

Military Service and Social Security
Publication No. 05-10017

Social Security: How You Earn Credits
Publication No. 05-10072
En Español: Publication No. 05-10972

*When You Retire from Your Own Business: What Social
    Security Needs to Know*
Publication No. 05-10038
En Español: Publication No. 05-10938

Medicare
Publication No. 05-10043
www.ssa.gov/pubs/10043.html
En Español: Publication No. 05-10943
www.ssa.gov/Espanol/10943.html

Receiving Your Benefits by Direct Deposit
Publication No. 05-10123
www.ssa.gov/pubs/10123.html
English and Spanish
En Español: Publication No. 05-10123
www.ssa.gov/Espanol/sp.html

Social Security Benefits for Children
Publication No. 05-10085
En Español: Publication No. 05-10985

Social Security: A Guide for Representative Payees
Publication No. 05-10076
En Español: Publication No. 05-10976
www.ssa.gov/ Espanol/10976.html

Social Security: Your Payments While You Are Outside the United States
Publication No. 05-10137
En Español: Publication No. 05-10138

The Social Security Statement: The Future's in Your Hands
Publication No. 05-10150
En Español: Publication No. 05-10150

Ticket to Work and Work Incentives Improvement Act of 1999
Publication No. 05-10133
www.ssa.gov/pubs/10133.html
Note: For publications in other languages, access
www.gov/multilanguage/

PUBLICATIONS IN SPANISH

Lista De Publicaciones En Español: Spanish Publications
Introducción al Programa de Seguro Social
Comprendiendo Los Beneficios 05-10924
Cómo Gana Usted Créditos 05-10972
Seguro Social: Cambios En 2001 05-10933
El Futuro del Seguro Social 05-10955
Beneficios Para Niños 05-10085
Una Instantánea del Seguro Social 05-10906
Cómo Ponerse En Contacto 05-10048sp
Sus Impuestos . . . Lo Que Están Pagando Y Donde Va El Dinero 05-10910

Servicio Telefónico de 24 horas 05-10982

Su Declaración de Seguro Social: El Futuro Está En Sus Manos 05-10150 (09/99)

Reciba Sus Beneficios Por Depósito Directo 05-10123

Días de Pago de Beneficios de Seguro Social En 1999 y 2000 05-10931

El Número de Seguro Social

Extranjeros Admitidos Legalmente—Cuándo Necesitan un número de Seguro Social y cuándo no lo necesitan 05-10996

Cuando Alguien Usa Su Número de Seguro Social Impropiamente 05-10964 (08/99)

Su Número Y Tarjeta 05-10902

Números para Recién Nacidos 05-10923

Beneficios de Jubilación

Cuando Usted Se Jubile de su Negocio Propio: Lo Que el Seguro Social Necesita Saber 05-10938

Lo Que Necesita Saber Si Recibe Beneficios por Jubilación o Sobrevivientes 05-10977

Beneficios de Jubilación 05-10935

Como Se Calcula Su Beneficio de Jubilación 05-10970

Una Pensión de Un Trabajo No Cubierto Por el Seguro Social 05-10945

Ajuste Por Pensión del Gobierno 05-10907

Beneficios de Sobrevivientes

Lo Que Necesita Saber Si Recibe Beneficios de Seguro Social por Jubilación o Sobrevivientes 05-10977

Sobrevivientes—Información General 05-10984

Beneficios de Incapacidad

Beneficios de Incapacidad—Información General 05-10929

El Programa del Boleto a Trabajar y la Autosuficiencia 05-10961

Trabajando Mientras Está Incapacitado—Una Guía Para Un Plan de Ayuda a Sí Sólo 05-10997

Beneficios para Niños con Incapacidades 05-10926
Definición de Incapacidad para Niños 05-11054
Guía de Beneficios Por Incapacidad de Seguro Social y SSI Para Personas con VIH 05-10920
Se Necesita Un Examen Especial Para Su Reclamación de Incapacidad 05-10987
Lo Que Debe Saber Si Recibe Beneficios de Seguro Social por Incapacidad 05-10903
Una Guía para Representantes de Beneficiarios 05-10976
Cómo Podemos Ayudarle Si Trabaja Mientras Está Incapacitado 05-10995
Revisión de Su Incapacidad 05-10968
Programas de Incapacidad de Seguro Social 05-10957
El Programa de Seguridad de Ingreso Suplementario (SSI) *Seguridad de Ingreso Suplementario* 05-11090
El Programa del Boleto a Trabajar y la Autosuficiencia 05-10961
¿Puede Usted Recibir SSI? 05-11070 (3/2001)
Seguridad de Ingreso Suplementario para Extranjeros 05-11052 (10/00)
Lo Que Necesita Saber Si Recibe Beneficios de SSI 05-11024
Trabajando Mientras Está Incapacitado—Una Guía Para Un Plan de Ayuda a Sí Sólo 05-10997
¿Su Derecho A Cuestionar La Decisión Hecha En Su Reclamación de SSI 05-11098
Beneficios para Niños con Incapacidades 05-10926
Definición de Incapacidad para Niños 05-11054
Guía de Beneficios Por Incapacidad de Seguro Social y SSI Para Personas con VIH 05-10920
Se Necesita Un Examen Especial Para Su Reclamación de Incapacidad 05-10987
Una Guía para Representantes de Beneficiarios 05-10976

Cómo Podemos Ayudarle Si Trabaja Mientras Está Incapacitado 05-10995

Revisión de Su Incapacidad 05-10968

Programas de Incapacidad de Seguro Social 05-10957

SSI Hojas de datos estatales (2001)

SSI en New York 05-11147

SSI en New Jersey 05-11149

SSI en el Estado de Washington 05-11105

SSI en California 05-11126

SSI en Massachusetts 05-11129

SSI en Nevada 05-11107

SSI Hojas de datos estatales (2000)

SSI en el Distrito de Columbia 05-11163

SSI en Pennsylvania 05-11151

Su Derecho de Apelación en el Seguro Social

El Proceso de Apelación 05-10941

El Seguro Social y Su Derecho a Representación 05-10975

Su Derecho a Cuestionar la Decisión Hecha en su Reclamación de Seguro Social 05-10958

Temas de Interés Particular

El Programa del Boleto a Trabajar y la Autosuficiencia 05-10961

Si Trabaja por Cuenta Propia 05-10922

Trabajadores Domésticos 05-10921

Cómo el Trabajo Afecta Sus Beneficios 05-10969

Cómo Se Calcula Su Beneficio de Jubilación 05-10970

Lo Que Toda Mujer Debe Saber 05-10927

Guía de Seguro Social para Agricultores, Cultivadores y Contratistas o Capataces 05-10925

Lo Que Deben Saber Los Prisioneros Sobre Seguro Social Anuncios Fraudulentos 05-10905

Sus Cheques de Seguro Social Durante Su Permanencia Fuera de los Estados Unidos 05-10138

Otros Programas Relacionados
Medicare 05-10943
Hechos Sobre Cupones de Alimentos 05-10105
Cupones de Alimentos y Otros Programas de Nutrición 05-10978
Lo Que Usted Necesita Saber sobre Medicare y Otros Seguros de Salud 05-10914
Información Importante sobre Medicaid 05-11042
Glosario de Términos de Seguro Social
Glosario Inglés-Español de Terminología del Seguro Social
Publicaciones Periódicas sobre la Administración de Seguro Social
Correo del Seguro Social

PUBLICATIONS IN OTHER LANGUAGES

The following publications are available by fax by calling toll-free 888-475-7000. The complete SSA Fax Catalog can be accessed at www.ssa.gov.

SSI in Hawaii (Japanese), Publication No. 05-11185
SSI in Hawaii (Tagalog), Publication No. 05-11186
Good News About SSI for Legal Immigrants (Chinese), Document No. 253
  (Hmong), Document No. 254
  (Korean), Document No. 255
  (Polish), Document No. 256
  (Russian), Document No. 257
  (Vietnamese), Document No. 258
SSI in California (Armenian), Publication No. 11182
SSI in California (Cambodian), Publication No. 11173
SSI in California (Chinese), Publication No. 11171
SSI in California (Farsi), Publication No. 11176

SSI in California (Hmong), Publication No. 11179

SSI in California (Japanese), Publication No. 11170

SSI in California (Korean), Publication No. 11177

SSI in California (Laotian), Publication No. 11184

SSI in California (Portuguese), Publication No. 11178

SSI in California (Punjabi), Publication No. 11183

SSI in California (Russian), Publication No. 11172

SSI in California (Tagalog), Publication No. 11181

SSI in California (Vietnamese), Publication No. 11180

Supplemental Security Income For Noncitizens (7/00); Publication No. 05-11051 (Armenian, Chinese, Haitian Creole, Hmong, Korean, Polish, Russian, Tagalog, and Vietnamese)

En Español Publication No. 05-11052

Good News About SSI for Certain Childhood Disability Recipients (Arabic, Cambodian, Chinese, English, Farsi, Haitian Creole, Korean)

SSI Benefits (Cambodian)

Social Security Disability Benefits (Cambodian)

SS-5 Completion Instruction (Russian)

The Future's in Your Hands (Polish translation of Publication No. 05-10150)

How Your Retirement Benefit Is Figured (Polish translation of Publication No. 05-10070)

Lawfully Admitted Aliens (Polish translation of Publication No. 05-10096)

A Snapshot (Polish translation of Publication 05-10006)

SSI—Supplemental Security Income (Polish) No. 249

Medicare Pays for Flu Shots (Polish) No. 250

Good News About SSI for Certain Childhood Disability Recipients (Laotian) (2/98) No. 295

Good News About SSI for Certain Childhood Disability Recipients (Polish) (2/98) No. 296

Good News About SSI for Certain Childhood Disability Recipients (Portugese) (2/98) No. 297

Good News About SSI for Certain Childhood Disability Recipients (Russian) (2/98) No. 298

Good News About SSI for Certain Childhood Disability Recipients (Vietnamese) (2/98) No. 299

Appendix V:
SOCIAL SECURITY Q & A

Q: Is it true that my Social Security benefits will be based on my highest five years of earnings?

A: No. For workers born after 1928, the SSA uses your best thirty-five years of earnings.

Q: Why can't I receive my Social Security Statement online?

A. The Social Security Administration suspended the interactive Social Security Statement test on April 9, 1997 because of concerns for safety, security, and privacy. Modified requests are being explored and another form of online statement may be offered in the future.

Q: My statement says my full retirement age is 66 years. I thought that everyone could retire at 65. Why is my retirement age different?

A. Previously, everyone needed to be age 65 or older to obtain full retirement benefits. However, the age of full retirement will gradually increase for those born in 1938 or later until it reaches 67 for people born after 1959. For example:

YEAR OF BIRTH	FULL RETIREMENT AGE
1937 or earlier	65
1938	65 and 2 months
1939	65 and 4 months
1940	65 and 6 months
1941	65 and 8 months
1942	65 and 10 months
1943–1954	66
1955	66 and 2 months
1956	66 and 4 months
1957	66 and 6 months
1958	66 and 8 months
1959	66 and 10 months
1960 and later	67

Q: Why is information about last year's earnings required?

A: Employers report wages on a yearly basis after the year is over. For 1999, employers were required to submit wage reports to Social Security by February 29, 2000. Social Security receives more than 260 million wage reports yearly and these reports are processed throughout the year.

Wage-posting activity for any previous tax year is completed by the end of the following year, and therefore, it is possible that the SSA has not yet posted your most recent earnings. By providing the SSA with the information, you will receive the most accurate benefit estimates that take into account your most recent earnings.

Q: My income comes from many different sources. How should I report this?

A: You are only credited with earnings on which you pay Social Security taxes, listed on employee paycheck stubs as FICA. If you are self-employed, the amount is noted on Schedule SE, which you attach to your 1040 personal income tax return.

CLUE: Earnings from interest, dividends, and unearned income are not included toward your credits. Regardless of your total earnings for a year, Social Security counts only earnings subject to FICA tax. The contribution and benefit base was $72,600 for wages paid in 1999 and self-employment income earned in taxable years beginning in 1999. Only the first $72,600 is taxed and only that amount is used in computing a benefit. For 2000, the maximum amount of taxable earnings for Social Security was $76,200.

Q: Is earnings information on the request form mandatory?

A: No. It is optional.

Q: I am a state employee not required to pay Social Security (FICA) taxes. What should I list on my form?

A: Nothing. Do *not* include any wages from state,

local, or federal government employment *not* covered for Social Security or covered *only* by Medicare.

Q: I retired at 55; what should I put in the block that reads "the age at which you PLAN to stop working"?

A: Age 55. The response you receive will give you a benefit estimate for three ages: 62, the minimum Social Security retirement age; your full retirement age; and age 70, the age you can draw benefits regardless of any continuous earnings from wages or self-employment.

Q: I want estimates of my retirement amount at several different ages, such as 62.5 years. How can I find out this information?

A: If you want to test different retirement ages, request one Social Security Statement and use the calculation program on the SSA Retirement Planner to figure out the benefits at different ages. You can access the planner at www.ssa.gov/retire. If you do not have access to a computer, call the SSA at 800-772-1213 and ask for a planner or for the SSA to do it for you.

Q: Why does the SSA need to know my mother's maiden name?

A: Your mother's maiden name was part of the information provided on your original application for a Social Security card, so it is a key to verifying your identity.

Q: Can I receive my statement in Spanish?

A: Yes. Just select that language at the beginning of the statement request page.

Q: What are the rules for listing addresses?

A: Abbreviate wherever possible. In the mailing address field, write in the actual street name including apartment numbers, suite numbers, P.O. box, etc. When the abbreviation *c/o* is applicable, use that field. For city, state, and zip code, write them in the specified fields. Avoid repetition. The foreign country field should be left blank.

For foreign addresses: The only information to be placed in the mailing address field is the street name, city, province, and postal code. The country goes in the foreign country field. The user's name and *c/o* information should be in the designated fields. City, state, and zip code are to be left blank.

Index

287

Index